Legendary GOLF CLUBS *of* Scotland, England, Wales and Ireland

Legendary GOLF CLUBS
of Scotland, England, Wales and Ireland

Photographed by
Anthony Edgeworth

Written by
John de St. Jorre

EDGEWORTH EDITIONS
Wellington, Florida

Preface

I wish that *Legendary Golf Clubs* had been written before my tour of some of them in 1987-88, as I could have been better prepared for that unlikely experience. Even without it then and having rather muddled through on my own, I now find this book delightful. It gives insights that enhance one's appreciation of some of these special places and people visited in person, and it gives fresh incentive to visit the others.

For such a treasure trove of information, impressions and human interest we are indebted to Anthony Edgeworth's keen photographic eye and John de St. Jorre's alertness to the histories of these uncommon clubs. Their careful preparation is here presented with perspective, sensitivity, eloquence and good humor.

While there is a wide variety of surroundings, both physical and aesthetic, enhancing these clubs and courses, there are certain shared themes and values that will be apparent to the reader visiting them vicariously. These similarities are both social, reflecting club members' attitudes, and sporting, as a love of golf is the common denominator.

The social dimension of the clubs has to do with the inclination of British gentlemen to share an enjoyment of club conviviality, such as permeates *Legendary Golf Clubs*. There may well be a broad variety of backgrounds within such a club's membership, but there is a certain like-mindedness about the club itself and the importance of preserving its traditions.

Of the individuals I have known who bear out this truism, the best example may be the late Bernard Darwin, whose fondness for golf club life was itself legendary, as he made clear in person and print.

The other essential element in such clubs is the members' love of golf. One's handicap is not a factor, so much as one's feel for the game and one's instinctive fraternal relationship with those who play it, all of whom share something rare. As John Updike puts it, "Golf camaraderie, like that of astronauts and Antarctic explorers, is based on a common experience of transcendence; fat or thin, scratch or duffer, we have been somewhere together where non-golfers never go."

Such a pure experience, and one's appreciation of it, is ageless, as it is the same for all golfers, always. I like to think that this timelessness allows each of us to claim a bit of immortality — surely the most valuable coin of the realm.

William C. Campbell
Huntington, West Virginia
August 1998

Introduction
A Way of Life

The men who founded the golf clubs in this book had much in common beyond a love of golf. They were nearly all socially prominent aristocrats, country gentry, lawyers, bankers or industrialists. Except for the founders of one earlier club, they all lived in the stratified society of late Victorian and Edwardian Britain. They were well-grounded in rural life, enjoyed country pursuits, and shared a passion for sport. Male companionship, whether in their city clubs, in pursuit of the fox, or playing golf together, was a major feature of their lives. They also had time on their hands and were constantly looking for ways to employ their leisure in companionable and entertaining ways.

Golf, which experienced a substantial expansion in the late nineteenth century, was perfectly suited to these men's social temperament and sporting inclinations. Here was a game that dovetailed with life-styles governed by an elaborate code of conduct: a game for gentlemen who instinctively did the proper thing.

They brought all this to the clubs they founded which were — and remain — intensely private institutions. But the founders also believed in the greater good of the game, and they played a critical role in promoting the early amateur and professional golf competitions. They organised, provided prizes and opened their courses for the tournaments and matches; they brought professionals, if not under their roofs, into their game as players and teachers. They also forged links with artisan clubs and other local golfers. This legacy lives on, in a most remarkable way, through the etiquette of golf — a game in which players still call penalties on themselves, do not toss their clubs around, and accept referees' decisions unquestioningly.

Memberships in these clubs are often continued from parent to child and with few exceptions, the acceptance of new members turns on how well they will fit in with existing members. Patterns of behaviour at the club set by the founders continue to this day, providing each club with its own traditional style: for some, foursomes, for others, four-ball; for some, a competitive game, for others, a more relaxed, social game; for some, elaborate luncheons, for others, simple sustenance; for some, elaborate club rooms, for others, the shelter of a modest bar.

A random glance at the scene in the Smoke Room, or Members Bar, of any club in this book will reveal how well tradition has been protected. You will observe an instinctive adherence to whatever the dress code may be, most often jacket and tie; a reverence for the club's history and personalities through its silver, portraits and honour boards; polite, efficient, and often long-serving staff; a close relationship among most members; a gracious hospitality towards their guests; and a deep, at times almost perverse respect for the physical fabric and furnishings of the clubhouse. The sounds and smells that evoke tradition live on: the crunch of spikes on gravel, the murmur of the caddies' voices as they wait to go out, the chink of glasses in the bar, the aroma of hot buttered toast, and the fragrance of pipe and cigar tobacco lingering among the ghosts of long-dead golfers after the last member has gone home.

Underpinning the trappings of tradition is the enduring love affair with the game of golf that these clubs have conducted for a century or more. Members rarely drop in just for a drink after work; they drop in for a game of golf. Which is not to say they are obsessed with how they play. The traditional preparation for a round at these clubs is several gentlemanly swipes with a driver on the first tee, without the pre-game practise ritual so typical, for example, in comparable American clubs.

Change, nevertheless, has taken place. Most of it has been wrought by economic and social factors originating far beyond the clubhouse. Private wealth may have been an unspoken assumed state among the founders. Today an important imperative for these clubs is to ensure that membership does not turn on having money, but rather on whether you are a desirable member. This means generating income from visitors, largely golfing societies' outings (in Britain a golfing society is a group of golfers, united by educational, professional or other interests, who play among themselves or against others on golf courses around the country). Another imperative is fulfilling what the clubs perceive as a duty, in their capacity as custodians of some of the world's greatest golf courses, to make them available, when possible, to the larger golfing community. Against these objectives must be balanced a third imperative, to preserve the particular private character of the club and to allow members to use the club as they wish.

The leisured days when many members could afford to spend more of their time on the links than in their offices are also gone. The pressure of work, of spouses and families who expect them home, and the speeding up of life in general, all mean less time at the club, although a number of members do preserve a multiplicity of clubs. The tightening noose of drink-driving laws has had a large impact on the social side of golf. Golfers drink less, and do not linger in the clubhouse as much as they once did.

Although a few secretaries who manage the clubs on a day-to-day basis may have wielded arbitrary powers in the past, that is no longer acceptable. But the clubs have always had a strong and continuing attachment to the creed of benevolent autocracy by one or a few leading members. "I believe all clubs need a measure of it," says a member of Royal County Down Golf Club. "If you are going to run things well, it can't be done too democratically. But the members must be kept happy, and that means looking after the course, the food and the ambience."

Most of these clubs have ladies' sections, although none of them have full, voting lady members. Both sexes, as a rule, seem comfortable with this arrangement, but there are exceptions. There is also some pressure to broaden the membership to people from different social, religious and racial backgrounds to those of the current membership. There is no knowing how strong these pressures may become. The clubs will probably find a way of working it out. "Change is perfectly all right as long as it is slow," says a senior member of Prestwick Golf Club. "It's all about speed, and it doesn't matter whether it is golf, politics or life in general. Nobody minds change, providing it doesn't alter one's life dramatically overnight."

With the growth and commercialisation of professional golf, traditional golf clubs have less direct influence on the sport, with the exception of the Royal and Ancient Golf Club of St. Andrews, which for much of the world has the final say on rules, equipment and amateur standing. These clubs do, however, continue to play an important part in preserving the sporting and gentlemanly style of golf through their dedication to managing their great courses, and through how they play the game. An experienced amateur golfer and close observer of the clubs summed it up: "They keep the culture of the game safe."

John de St. Jorre
Mallorca, Spain
July 1998

Published by Edgeworth Editions
Copyright © 1998 by Edgeworth Editions
Photographs copyright © by Anthony Edgeworth
Text copyright © by John de St. Jorre

This book was produced by
CommonPlace Books, New Canaan, Connecticut
Art Director: Samuel N. Antupit
Editor: Paul De Angelis
Production Design: Cheung/Crowell Design

The photographs for this book were taken with Canon cameras using lenses ranging in size from 20mm to 600mm. Photographs were taken on 35mm Ektachrome and Kodachrome film provided by Eastman Kodak.

Printed in Hong Kong through Global Interprint

ISBN # 0-9658904-1-4 — Library of Congress Card #98-073774

All rights reserved. This book, or any portions thereof, may not be reproduced in any form without written permission from the publisher.

Further copies of this book may be ordered by calling 1-877-360-golf or through the Internet at www.greatgolfcourses.com. Any inquiries should be directed to:

Edgeworth Editions
2134 Polo Gardens Drive
Suite 104
Wellington, FL 33414
USA

Previous pages:

Lining up a putt, Royal Worlington and Newmarket.

Silver championship trophy, Porthcawl.

A good out at Swinley Forest.

St. George's links moonscape.

Silver and gold captains' balls (detail), R&A.

Father and son in Royal Norfolk's Smoke Room.

Members and golfing friends in the dining room beneath the portrait of William Laidlaw Purves, founder of St. George's.

Putting out on the 11th tee at Liverpool.

Late afternoon putt at Rye.

Contents

11 *Preface*
by William C. Campbell

13 *Introduction*
A Way of Life

SCOTLAND

22 *Golf's Alma Mater*
Royal and Ancient
Golf Club of St. Andrews

58 *A Day's Fun*
Prestwick Golf Club

78 *Kummel:*
The Putting Mixture

ENGLAND

80 *Breeder of Mighty*
Champions
Royal Liverpool
Golf Club

104 *An Heroic Course*
The Royal St. George's
Golf Club

130 *Club Grub*

132 *Ah, Rye!*
Rye Golf Club

152 *A Golfer's Club*
Sunningdale Golf Club

176 *A Haven for Golfing*
Gentlemen
Swinley Forest Golf Club

196 *Clean, Sober and Wise:*
The Caddie

198 *A Nine-Hole Wonder*
Royal Worlington
and Newmarket Golf Club

218 *A Family Affair*
Royal West Norfolk
Golf Club

WALES

242 *A Hidden Gem*
Royal Porthcawl
Golf Club

IRELAND

262 *Are You in the Hat Today?*
The Royal County Down
Golf Club

284 *Sanctuary*
Portmarnock Golf Club

306 *Capital Golfers*
The Golf Match Club

310 *Club Addresses*

312 *Acknowledgments*

Golf's Alma Mater

Royal and Ancient Golf Club of St. Andrews

St. Andrews, Scotland, September 1997: In the uncertain light of dawn, St. Andrews could still be a medieval city. The grey stone walls protecting it from the sea loom large; the arcaded quadrangles of learning are peaceful; and cobbled streets magnify the sound of early morning feet. This was once Scotland's greatest city, the cradle of its religion and the birthplace of its first university. As the light strengthens, the town's Victorian face emerges — a neo-gothic countenance of angular grey stone and red brick buildings.

A clock strikes the hour. Down near the sea a cluster of spectators tenses expectantly behind the 1st tee of the Old Course of the public golf links on which golf has been played for more than 500 years. On the tee stands a true Scotsman, immaculately attired in plus-fours, a dark green waistcoat, a tweed jacket, matching cap and the Club tie of the Royal & Ancient Golf Club of St. Andrews, known by golfers everywhere simply as the R&A. He addresses the ball briefly, swings his club and drives firmly down the fairway. The cannon to his right booms out, perfectly synchronised and drowning the satisfactory sound of a well-struck golf ball. The ball lifts into the wind and falls a little to the left of centre. There is a mad scamper of the waiting caddies and one of the younger ones dives and retrieves the ball. He approaches the golfer who hands him a gold sovereign in exchange for the ball. The photo opportunity is taken, hands are shaken and the crowd applauds. Sandy Mathewson, the new Captain of the R&A, has just driven himself in.

Behind the spectators stands a solid, imposing building of mellow sandstone, sited on a small plateau from which it commands untrammelled views of the Old Course and St. Andrews Bay. Built largely at the height of British imperial power in the nineteenth century, the R&A's clubhouse is surely the most recognisable golf edifice in the world. The British Empire has gone, but the R&A's hegemony over the ever-expanding game of golf flourishes. And the body and soul of this sporting raj reside here.

The inside of the clubhouse is no less imposing and reflects the Club's position in the governance of the game. A spacious entrance hall, aglow with wood and flowers on a table, contains ceremonial lockers with the names of prominent members such as Gene

Sarazen, Peter Thomson, Gary Player, Kel Nagle, Roberto DeVicenzo, Jack Nicklaus and other distinguished members. To the right, behind a reception desk, stands the hall porter, Bob Marshall, to direct or inform guests and respond to the members' every need.

The adjacent Trophy Room exhibits the crown jewels of golf including the ornate Moroccan leather and silver belt that was the prize for the first decade of the Open Championship; the silver Claret Jug which succeeded it; the Amateur Championship trophy; and the silver club to which each new Captain of the R&A adds a silver ball. The names associated with these trophies include nearly every great golfer in the last century and a half, a representation of golfing legend sufficient to send a chill of excitement down the most unsentimental of spines.

The principal room in the clubhouse is appropriately called the Big Room. It is a large, well-proportioned space with opposing open fireplaces and a generous bow window which overlooks the Old Course. Around the lower walls are more, largely ceremonial lockers assigned to the most senior members of the Club, surmounted by a veritable art gallery that includes splendid portraits of the Queen, the R&A's patron; her uncle Edward VIII, who as Prince of Wales was Captain in 1922; and Old Tom Morris, Custodian of the Links for many decades.

Then there is a library, containing a large and varied collection of books on every aspect of the game and doubling as a card-room; a sitting-room; a committee room, and upstairs the dining room. Upstairs are also offices, some of which may soon be moved to newly-acquired property outside the clubhouse, and the Secretary's Office, with its balcony and the best view of the links in the entire clubhouse. In the basement are the members' changing room and the snooker and billiard room.

Founded in 1754 by twenty-two noblemen and gentlemen of Fife, the R&A is one of the very oldest golf clubs in the world. In the first seventy years or so of its life "the Society of St. Andrews Golfers", as they called themselves, was a loose-knit organisation that played annually for a silver club, the winner becoming the "Captain of the Golf" for the next year. The Club did not have a clubhouse and shared the public links, then as now, with the citizens of St. Andrews.

By 1824 it had been decided that golfing prowess was not always the best way to choose a Captain, but the fiction of the competition has been preserved by the custom of the new Captain driving himself in and, as the only entry, "winning" the silver club and the Queen Adelaide medal. Ten years later King William IV became the Club's patron and conferred upon it the resonant and prestigious title of "Royal and Ancient Golf Club of St. Andrews".

The original rules of golf — thirteen of them — were drawn up in 1744 by the Gentlemen Golfers at Leith when they formed the first golf club (now the Honourable Company of Edinburgh Golfers), and were adopted by their counterparts in St. Andrews. Until the 1830s both groups were generally acknowledged by golfers as custodians of the game's rules and traditions. But then the Leith golfers suffered what Keith Mackie's official booklet, *The Royal and Ancient Golf Club of St. Andrews*, delicately calls "a temporary loss of cohesion", and the R&A "without conscious exercise of authority, gradually acquired the status of premier club."

Notwithstanding the R&A's informal position as "first" among golf clubs, the editor of

Previous pages:
Former captain of the R&A with Ladies' Putting Club member at St. Andrews.
Opposite:
Silver club detail.

Following pages:
The town of St. Andrews.
Spectators await the driving-in of the new captain at the Autumn Meeting.

The crown jewels of golf (left to right): The (Queen Victoria) Jubilee Vase; the Amateur Championship Trophy; the Claret Jug (Open Championship Trophy); and the Calcutta Cup. At bottom, the Championship Belt and the silver club with captains' balls.

Dr. A. M. (Sandy) Mathewson, captain of the R&A (1997-98).

Golf Magazine could note as late as 1891: "Almost alone among high-class sports, golf stands out as a conspicuous example of a difficult and intricate game played by thousands of our educated classes absolutely without organisation, with no cohesion among the body of the players, with no code of rules made by duly accredited representatives of golf as a whole."

Such informality might have sufficed forever, had the game continued to involve only "thousands" at tradition-minded clubs like those portrayed in this book. But by the end of the nineteenth century golf had become a popular game in a number of countries and uniformity of the rules was needed. So the golf clubs of the time turned to the R&A to provide a unified code.

In response, the R&A appointed its first Rules of Golf Committee in 1897 and was, thenceforward, recognised as the governing body for the rules of the sport throughout the world except for the USA, which run their own affairs under the aegis of the United States Golf Association (USGA). Cooperation over the years between the R&A and the USGA has gradually made this exception largely meaningless as far as the rules are concerned. "When I first came to St. Andrews in 1950," says Bill Campbell, an American who has the distinction of having served both as Captain of the R&A and president of the USGA, "I was given nine typewritten pages of differences between the R&A and USGA codes. It wasn't until January 1984," he says, "when I happened to be president of the USGA, that we finally produced uniformity in the rules. And it was even later that a joint decision book interpreting the rules was issued."

A second major development for the R&A came in 1920 when Britain's leading golf clubs asked it to take over the running of the Open and Amateur Championships, a nation-wide task that has expanded over the years to include the staging of the Boys, Mid-Amateur and Seniors Championships, as well as the selection of the teams to represent Britain and Ireland in such events as the World Amateur Team Championship, the Walker Cup and the St. Andrews Trophy, a biennial match between Britain/Ireland and continental Europe. This historical process of having responsibility thrust upon it, rather than acquiring it of its own volition, is undoubtedly one of the sources of the R&A's strength and prestige today.

"We never sought or were appointed by anybody to be the governing authority of the rules of golf," says Sir Michael Bonallack, the R&A's present Secretary and one of the game's great amateur players. "It was the same with the Open and Amateur Championships and things like amateur status. We do them by consent and it's probably the best way."

Sir Michael believes that one of the strengths of the R&A, and of golf as a rapidly growing international sport, is that the rules are supervised by a body that has no commercial interest in the game: in short, by a group of amateur golfers organised in a private members' club. "You usually find that most sports suffer," he says, "when the ruling bodies are made up of the same people who are playing the game for money." He says that the professional golf tours strongly approve of the R&A being in charge of the rules, although they have an input into the reviewing process. "They've told us time and time again they don't want to be rule-makers, just rule-enforcers."

These responsibilities are carried out because of the willingness of the members to

Opposite top: *Robertson (Bob) Marshall, hall porter.* Opposite: *Copper sign on clubhouse wall.*

contribute countless hours working on Club committees appropriately named "Rules," "Implements and Ball," "Amateur Status," "Championship," and the relatively new, less precisely named "External Fund Supervisory Committee", which distributes the large profits made out of the Open for the benefit of golf wherever it may be played. The committees are ably supported by the Secretary, the Rules, Championship, Finance and Members' Secretaries, and Assistant Secretaries who carry out the day-to-day work. All of this functions under the General Committee, which is the governing and policy body of the Club. The significant actions of the committees are reported to all members in meticulous reports and minutes at the twice-yearly members' meetings. The latter are well attended and often pro forma. But occasionally there is some debate both on the game's governance and on the private activities of the Club . . . as well as good humour, such as a senior member's enquiry as to whether the Big Room should retain its name when renovations shortened it by twenty inches.

The limits and purpose of this book preclude a serious description of the full contribution of the R&A to golf, but a few details will give a sense of its diverse activities.

Four million copies of the rules in English are circulated every year and are also published in twenty other languages. The R&A booklet reports that "some 3,000 obscure, complicated and sometimes hilarious enquiries" on the rules reach the R&A annually.

The Implements and Ball Committee has to grapple with issues associated with technological advance and the evolution of the modern game. "One of the problems is that the ball is going much further than it used to," says Bonallack, "and it is tending to make a lot of the old championship courses obsolete. Nobody is quite sure why. . . It could be the ball itself, the new clubs with their graphite shafts and titanium heads, or the players, who are fitter, stronger and better trained than in the past. Or it could be a mixture of all these things."

"We make quite a lot of money out of the Open Championship," says Richard Cole-Hamilton, past chairman of the General Committee. "In 1996 about £5.4 million went out to deserving causes and in 1997 roughly £6 million. The sort of thing we fund includes the Golf Foundation for coaching at 2,500 schools throughout Britain, clubs that want to build new holes and put in watering systems (but not for repairs to clubhouses), professionals to go out to places like India or Slovenia to develop their golf, supporting the building of public links courses, and helping the European Golf Association with their tournaments."

Thus from its ancient beginnings as a Scottish club for the notables of St. Andrews and the surrounding countryside, the R&A has evolved into a complex and powerful international organisation in what is arguably the world's most widespread and popular sport. This makes it very different from the rest of the legendary clubs portrayed in this book.

Behind this sophisticated governing edifice, the R&A remains as it was from the beginning, a private men's golf club. More than 600 members make the annual pilgrim-

Opposite top: *Sir Michael Bonallack on the Club Balcony.* Opposite: *Secretary's office.*

Following pages:
The Big Room overlooking the 1st tee, Old Course.
A pitch and run to the 18th, Old Course.

A Big Room detail.

age to the Club's Autumn Meeting to play golf and enjoy the exceptional camaraderie which the game fosters. The Club's total membership is 1800, with 1050 from Britain and Ireland (less than 100 are St. Andrews residents) and the balance, 750, from overseas. The overseas membership has a historical quota system, with the United States having 275 members, the old Commonwealth countries 110 and other countries a top limit of 50 each. For most people the R&A is not a first club but a place to join later. Sir Michael notes that the clubhouse has "a complete cross-section of people — former heads of state and leaders of government like George Bush and Kenneth Kaunda, veteran politicians like Lord Whitelaw, who was Mrs. Thatcher's deputy prime minister, film stars such as Sean Connery, prominent figures in other sports including racing drivers Jackie Stewart and Nigel Mansell, business leaders and amateurs working for the professional golf tours. It's a very interesting club because you never know who you are going to meet."

Over the years forty-three Open Champions — from John Ball who won in 1890 to Robert Tyre Jones, Jr. in 1930, to Bobby Locke in 1957, to Jack Nicklaus in 1978, have become members; while fifty-six Amateur Champions — from Allan MacFrie in 1885, to Cyril Tolley in 1920, to Michael Bonallack in 1961, to Peter McEvoy in 1978 — have been or become members. Captains from William Landale in 1754 to Dr. Alexander Mathewson in 1997 include the Prince of Wales (1863 and 1902); the Duke of York

Members of the General Committee.

(1930); the Duke of Kent (1937); and such golf luminaries as Horace Hutchinson (1908), Bernard Darwin (1934), Roger Wethered (1946) and Francis Ouimet (1951).

To become a member of this unique institution you have to be invited, proposed and seconded and have sufficient support from members within the Club. A candidate has to show that he is interested in golf, that he will use the Club, be ready to serve on the committees and be a good, sociable companion for other members — the sort of person you would like to play golf with. There is no handicap limit for R&A membership — future members are expected to have a reasonable standard of golf — and the waiting period to be elected is about five years.

The small nucleus who live within the St. Andrews area form the core of the Club during the late autumn, winter and early spring. There are various Club team matches mostly against the Scottish clubs or societies, and occasional lunches and dinners which include lady guests. But the great times for most of the membership are the May Spring Meeting, the month of August, and the September Autumn Meeting, when the clubhouse overflows with members from the four corners of the earth.

At these times there are members who have not seen each other for a number of years, members who played each other last week at another of their clubs, and some members who are meeting for the first time. With glass or tankard in hand, they move in and out of the Big Room. There is no bar in the clubhouse, but extraordinarily quick and

Following pages: *St. Andrews links.*

Clockwise from top left: T. H. (Harvey) Douglas, past captain, with Dr. A. M. (Sandy) Mathewson, new captain, September 1997; P. F. (Peter) Gardiner-Hill, former captain of the R&A and Mel Dickenson, president of Pine Valley Golf Club; Relief Porter John Gillespie (left)

and Assistant Porter Ford Horsfield with the Silver Club and other trophies; detail of the Open Championship belt; three American members at the Fall Meeting; stairway to the Secretary's office. Above: The Big Room; scales; hand-towels.

Above and opposite: *The Claret Jug* (details).

Troon, July 1997

From early in the morning until the light fades over the Irish Sea, a vast throng of men, women and children ebbs and flows across the links. High winds and marauding showers of fine Celtic rain, blowing in from the west, bring forth a forest of multi-coloured umbrellas and prompt some good-humoured comments. Clusters of tents with conical tops and fluttering banners, towering gantries and miles of electric cables suggest that a medieval battle for a Hollywood epic is about to be filmed. But the epic in question is the countdown for the star turn on the British golfing calendar, the Open Championship, which is about to take place here at the Royal Troon Golf Club on the west coast of Scotland.

While there is a sense of purpose and discipline about the build-up, it is hard to discern a guiding hand. It is rather like being on a great ocean liner, steaming sedately across an empty ocean, engines throbbing somewhere down below but no sign of anyone up on the bridge. However, now and again in the crowds, among the makeshift Portacabin offices, or on the course, you will catch sight of men in navy blue blazers, white shirts, discreet Club ties and small red rosettes in their lapels. They are officials of the R&A, responsible for running this great sporting event, and they handle it superbly — efficiently, impartially and discreetly.

Peter Greenhough, chairman of the R&A's Championship Committee, briefs the officials who will be refereeing and

cheerful waitresses and waiters stand ready at the end of a bell to deliver yet another libation. At the Spring and Fall Meetings, results of the various members' competitions for beautifully designed trophies bearing such exotic names as the Kangaroo's Paw, the Silver Boomerang, the Calcutta Cup, the Silver Beaver, the Jubilee Vase, the Manaia trophy, and the Pine Valley Plate, are posted on newspaper-size sheets in the Big Room and in the Front Hall. Amid the constant movement can be heard much laughter and the explosive cries of long-delayed reunions. For those who have arranged early tee times in the competitions, or have been eliminated, there are lunches with claret and port in the upstairs dining room. Black-tie dinners, often over-subscribed, are held on various evenings.

The Spring Meeting lasts for a week but the Autumn Meeting is spread over three weeks in September. The first week is for knock-out foursomes; the second week, knock-out matchplay singles; and the third week has four days of medal play and also the traditional putting competition when former R&A Captains compete with members of the Ladies' Putting Club over the Himalayas, an 18-hole putting course situated between the Old Course and St. Andrews Bay. The Autumn Meeting now also includes a cocktail party for members and their ladies, a mixed foursome event and the ritual annual dinner in the Town Hall.

It is also a time when Club and town battle, in a sporting fashion, in what is probably the world's largest golf match. The R&A take on all the other golf clubs in St.

administering the competition. Most of them are R&A members, but some are guests from other golfing organisations. Amid the sea of male faces are three women. Greenhough covers a range of items: how far press photographers are allowed in front of the ropes (an arm's length); how to deal with the slow play, the *bête noire* of the modern game (impose stroke penalties for "bad times" and disqualify the player after four offences).

David Rickman, Rules Secretary, runs through the local Troon rules and other issues such as the problem that balls become enmeshed in the intricacies of the TIO's — "temporary immovable obstructions" such as grandstands, TV towers and leader-boards. These unplayable balls were last year's biggest headache.

Anyone who has a dispute with a player (who, it is emphasised, is not entitled to a second opinion), or any other doubts, is to call in the "rover". "It is not a sign of weakness," David Rickman says, "but a sign of good judgement."

Ian Webb, the chairman-elect of the R&A's General Committee, explains the role of the four rovers. "As a referee I would give my judgement, but in exceptional circumstances I would call in a rover who, hopefully, would confirm my decision. However, the main duty of the rovers is to maintain the pace of play."

All is ready, the sun has broken through the veil of cloud over the Isle of Arran, and tomorrow the 126th Open Championship will begin.

Overleaf:
Rules Committee, Open Championship, Troon, July

Following pages: *Old Course fairway. Golfers approaching the 18th green on the Old Course.*

Andrews in a day-long competition, involving 360 players on each side, over the Old and New Courses. This match symbolises what is now an amicable relationship between Club and town.

In the past there had been conflict between the town and the Club, particularly about control of the Old Course. Today, an independent body called the St. Andrews Links Trust, composed of local government and Club nominees, controls the links, which are managed by four R&A appointees and four Fife Council appointees. The R&A does enjoy certain preferred times of play, especially during the Spring and Autumn Meetings. The fact that the R&A does not own any of the five 18-hole and one 9-hole courses that twist and turn along the linksland between town and bay, although an anomaly, somehow adds to its regal position in the world of golf.

The Old Course, which was the only course until the New Course was built in 1896 and the Jubilee Course was built in 1897, is where golf has been played since time immemorial. Once 12 holes, then 22, by 1764 the Old Course had fixed the number of holes at 18. It is famous for its shared double greens on all but 4 holes, and its natural but devilish bunkers such as the Principal's Nose, Strath, Hill, Mrs. Kruger, Beardies and Hell. Two holes are named after two of golf's greatest figures, Tom Morris, number 18 and Bobby Jones, number 10. Then there is perhaps the most famous hole in golf, hole 17, simply named the Road Hole because of where

it is. The Old Course is where every golfer wants to play before he dies.

An interesting historical aside about the Old Course is that up until World War I it was regularly played in reverse from the 1st tee to the 17th green, from the 18th tee to the 16th green and so on, on alternate weeks. This may be the source of "backwards tournaments" adopted by some other clubs.

Being Captain of the R&A is one of the most prestigious positions in the sport's hierarchy. Most ancient institutions seem to preserve an air of mystery about how they select their leaders, and the R&A is no exception. In December every year, the past Captains gather in a hotel in London and narrow down a short-list of people they have prepared earlier and select a name. They disperse and somewhere in a golfing home, somewhere around the world, the telephone rings and the question is popped. "Would you accept the nomination of captaincy of the R&A for the next year?"

According to firsthand accounts from some of them, the recipient of the call is invariably "flabbergasted". Here are some impressions about the job from several past Captains — one American, two Irish and two English:

Bill Campbell [1987–88]: "I was the third American to have the job, after Francis Ouimet (1955–56) and Joseph Dey (1979–80). I was thunderstruck because it was totally beyond my expectations and I didn't even call my wife about it. Just went home that night from work and she was seated by the fire, sewing, and I said, 'Guess what happened today.' Without a flicker of hesitation, she said, '*Let's* do it.' So it was a joint venture.

"As Captain you don't run anything, you're the spokesman, the symbol of the R&A. Marvellous traditions like the Captain driving-in at the hour that used to be set for executions in Britain. . . . It's a total experience, something you can only dream about."

Joe Carr [1991–92]: "What really amazed me was the awe and love that golf clubs around the world have for the R&A, even in America where it does not govern anything. The former Captains pick the new one. There are about twenty of us left and we meet twice during the year to consider candidates and then we all go over to London in December to pick one. Each candidate is fully discussed, and when I heard that the first time, I said, 'Thank God I wasn't here last year to hear you talk about me!'"

Harry McCaw [1995–96]: "It took me completely by surprise but it was a great honour. The R&A is really run by the Chairman of the General Committee and the Secretary, who is the chief executive, if you will, reporting to the General Committee. This leaves the Captain in an ambassadorial role, representing the game of golf in an ethereal sense."

John Behrend [1984–85]: "In my time there was no initial telephone call, just a letter marked 'private and confidential'. When I saw it I thought, I've forgotten to pay my subscription. Although I was apprehensive, it's not the thing you say no to. Of course, you never forget the morning you drive in. In my case it was very dramatic. I walked up to the ball and did what I normally do when playing golf, took a practise swing about a foot away from the ball. The cannon went off, so technically it was an air shot. Everybody burst out laughing. Anyway, it relieved the tension and then I drove off. Afterwards Gerald Micklem came up to me and shook my hand and said in that brusque tone of his: 'Well, that was two firsts, Behrend.' Not only had the gunner mistaken my practise swing for the real thing, but I was not wearing a tie."

Peter Gardiner-Hill [1982-83]: "As honorary secretary of the past Captains' group, it's my job to make the telephone call. Having done it four or five times now, I've got used to the shock that everybody feels, including myself, when asked the question. My job is to secure the agreement of the person. I encourage him to talk to friends among the past Captains. We are always looking for candidates who are representative of the world-wide spectrum of golf. This is where we are different from the USGA because they could never have a president from outside the United States."

"Captains have tended to fall into three categories," says John Behrend who, together with Peter Lewis, the director of the British Golf Museum, is writing an official history of the R&A. "There are the prominent locals from St. Andrews and Fife; people who have contributed to the Club through work on its committees; and outstanding figures in the world of golf or society at large."

The light dissolves slowly over the links and the wind slackens. The lone piper on the sea-front, who has been entertaining the sightseers all afternoon, plays a last lament. The clubhouse which, in the grey light of an autumn day, resembled nothing as much as a stern Victorian dowager presiding over a debutante ball, is softened by dusk and becomes congenial as the lights go on and the members gather for drinks before the dinner at the Town Hall.

St. Andrews, with its stone walls, its ruined cathedral which once ruled the Scottish church, its cobbled streets and ancient university, is settling down for the night. Golf was almost certainly being played here when the university was founded in the early fifteenth century. The game's first recorded appearance came, ironically, with a ban by a Scottish king, who thought the locals should be practising their archery instead of their putting. Its enduring quality, even that long ago, was proven when another king in another century granted the citizens of St. Andrews the use of the links for their pleasure to disport themselves at "golff, futball and schuting."

By the time the local golfers formed their Club in the middle of the eighteenth century, St. Andrews was already recognised as the alma mater of the game. And over the centuries, kings, at least one queen (Mary Queen of Scots), bishops, ambassadors, professors and other dignitaries have played up and down the strand, struggling with the game, the elements and themselves, just as members and their guests at the Autumn Meeting have done today.

At the Town Hall, the annual dinner is under way. Members from all over the world are there, side-by-side, eating good food, drinking drinkable wine and enjoying the special brotherhood that is as much part of the game as club and ball. The outgoing Captain introduces the new incumbent who answers; a respected figure toasts the new members and a representative of the initiates responds. After the speeches, the Captain holds up the silver club laden with silver balls. The new members come forward and one by one, kiss one of the balls, a symbolic act making them full members.

Outside the wind is gathering strength again, rattling the whins on the links and skirmishing with the sand on the broad beaches where the unforgettable opening sequence of *Chariots of Fire* was filmed. Tomorrow will be another challenging day of golf on this ancient linksland and there is no doubt that the game is in safe hands.

Prestwick Golf Club

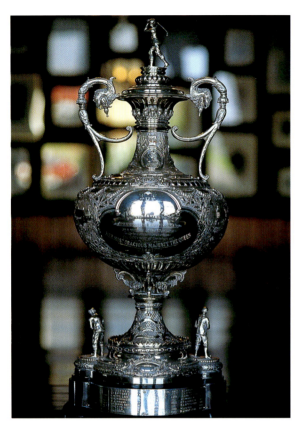

Saturday, 12.30 pm. A blustery autumn day, with fluffy white clouds scudding in from the Firth of Clyde over the Prestwick links in Ayrshire, western Scotland. Inside the clubhouse, the staff are putting the final touches to the luncheon table. For a moment the Club dining-room is empty, a good opportunity to contemplate the dressed table, a minor work of art as seductive to the visual senses as it is appealing to the appetite.

A single, solid, gleaming mahogany table almost fills the room. Thirty-two dark green place mats, bearing the Club's crest of two crossed golf clubs, three balls, the name "Prestwick" and the date "1851", are perfectly aligned, like Guardsmen on parade. Along the centre are the grace notes for the meal to come: silver cruet, small plates of oatcakes and Ryvita crackers, Lea & Perrins Worcestershire sauce, Sharwoods mango chutney, Major Macdonald's Regimental Chilli tomato relish, Arran mustard, more chutneys and horseradish sauce on open dishes with long silver spoons; and whole, freshly-baked ginger and fruit cakes, with sharp knives at their side, biding their time. Wine, water and port glasses accompany each place-setting, and bottles of the Club claret and glass water jugs are interspersed at even intervals the length of the table.

On an oak sideboard, which looks like a medieval artefact liberated from a monastery, is spread a cold buffet: a trencherman's rib of beef weighing in at around twenty pounds, fresh tongue, and a boiled Belfast ham. Not far away is the cheeseboard, sunken in a green tiled trough, offering a whole Stilton wrapped in a starched white napkin, Cheddar, Cheshire and Boursault; alongside, adding a splash of colour, are a jug of fresh celery and small dishes of strawberries, grapes and dates.

The lower walls of the room are wood-panelled, the upper painted a dark green. Around the room are portraits of past Captains. Pride of place is given to the thirteenth Earl of Eglinton, the land-owning aristocrat who founded Prestwick in 1851; his gaze is met on the opposite wall by that of Charles Hunter, "Keeper of the Green" and the Club's longest serving professional. The Club silver, laid out on either side of the Victoria Vase, is displayed on the mantelpiece. This elegant, intimate dining-room is the heart and soul of the Prestwick Golf Club.

The room soon fills up with members and their guests and in no time a visitor is put at ease. The choice of starters includes a seafood platter consisting of lobster, langoustines, mussels, scallops, oysters, smoked salmon and caviar; or a plate of delicious and surprisingly delicate haggis dumplings served with a mustard and cream sauce; or a choice of freshly-made soups. This is followed by a selection of roast beef, lamb, baked ham, braised oxtails, kidneys, pheasant, steak and kidney pudding or curry — plus the alternative of the cold buffet.

Prestwick's long table, unusual in the world of traditional golf clubs, is symbolic of this Club's custom that no member should be left out of the Club's pleasures whether they involve golfing, drinking, or eating. For Club members it is as important as the round table was to King Arthur and his knights. For the guest, Saturday lunch provides a privileged insight into what this historic Club is all about. The dining-room may be part of the Club's inner sanctum, but it is not sacrosanct; any guest may enter and sample both the good victuals and the human warmth of this group of men. When asked what it means to the members to come down to Prestwick on a Saturday for a couple of rounds of golf, a few drinks and a super lunch, the answer is invariably that they come to escape the cares of everyday life and to enjoy themselves. They come, from far and wide, for a day's fun.

Behind the fun lies almost a century and half of history. The Club's informative and elegant history, *Prestwick Golf Club: Birthplace of the Open*, edited by David Smail, records its genesis: "The Club was formed by a group of like-minded men, who met on 2 July 1851, in the Red Lion Hotel, Prestwick, happily still standing. As with the founders of the R&A and the Honourable Company, these men were men of property, pillars of the community, the landed gentry — indeed nobility — and men of the services and professions. It was not so much that they were men of wealth, but men of leisure, men who had time for golf and other country pursuits."

Two developments hastened the spread of golf around the time of Prestwick's foundation in the mid-nineteenth century. First was the replacement of the "feathery" ball by the gutta-percha ball, which travelled a great deal farther and was much cheaper to produce. Second was the rapid expansion of Britain's railway system, which helped to open up the coast of Ayrshire to golfers who, taking advantage of the natural links terrain, established golf clubs first at Prestwick and, later, at Gailes, Barassie, Troon and Turnberry.

The original 12-hole course at Prestwick was bounded on the south by the Links Road which connects the town with the beach, the railway line on the east, the sea on the west, and by Pow Burn and the Wall which ran across to the beach. The Wall later disappeared, as the course was extended northward to accommodate 18 holes; but the other boundaries remain intact.

The key figure in Prestwick's early days was Colonel James Ogilvie Fairlie, a golfing companion and close friend of the Earl of Eglinton. Fairlie, who had been Captain of the R&A the year before Prestwick's creation, quickly mustered a sizeable membership for the new Club (entrance fee: £1; annual subscription: £1). He

Previous pages:
Prestwick's challenging course, where the first Open Championship was played.
Opposite:
The Victoria Vase.

Following pages:
View of the 4th hole and 12th fairway with Pow Burn in foreground. Dining-room, Saturday lunch, presided over by the Earl of Eglinton, Club founder.

arranged for Old Tom Morris, the leading golfer of the day, to come across from St. Andrews to complete the laying out of the course and be "Keeper of the Green". Morris brought with him his infant son, Tom, who was to grow up on the Prestwick links and become one of the game's great champions.

Nine years after the foundation of the Club, Prestwick was responsible for organising and holding the first Open Championship. In 1856 the Club had proposed a medal play tournament of 36 holes open to professionals from all golf clubs, to be played at either St. Andrews or Prestwick. The reaction from other clubs was lukewarm, so Prestwick decided to go it alone. As a prize, the Club commissioned a handsome red leather belt with a large silver buckle depicting golfers and caddies, at the cost of £25. Anyone winning the belt for three successive years could keep it. Letters were sent out to golf clubs in Scotland and England inviting them to send no more than three of their best professionals to the competition; Prestwick's invitation made the point that "the players must be known and respected cadies".

The first Open consisted of three rounds on 17 October 1860 over Prestwick's 12-hole course. As dusk fell, Willie Park emerged the victor. According to the Club history: "No doubt, on the next day, the Prestwick Medal Day, the really important day at Prestwick, most of the contestants once more reverted to being honest 'cadies'".

The Open was held at Prestwick every year for the next decade. In 1870 Young Tom Morris scored his third successive victory, and permanently retired the Belt. Thereafter the Open winner received the Challenge Trophy, which is always passed on. Prestwick went on to hold a total of twenty-four Opens, producing such great champions as Willie Auchterlonie, Harry Vardon and James Braid. Its last Open was held in 1925 when Jim Barnes of the United States won it by a stroke with a total of 300 for 72 holes.

Since then Prestwick has largely confined its activities to amateur golf. The Amateur Championship has been held there sixteen times and will return in the year 2001, the Club's 150th anniversary. Other championships fought out over these wind-swept links include the Boys and the Seniors Amateur. Like several other famous traditional golf clubs, Prestwick cannot cope with the crowds and the impedimenta of the modern Open. "I would like to think that we will host the home internationals again," says Ian Bunch, the Club's Secretary, "and perhaps a Walker or Curtis Cup. We can certainly accommodate them."

Bernard Darwin liked holes to have names, to render them human. "Hole and bunkers that can bring down great men with so terrible a crash deserve great names," he wrote, "and in these Prestwick is rich." With names like the Himalayas, the Alps, the Sahara, the Railway, the Tunnel, and the Bridge, golfers new to Prestwick have a pretty good idea of what awaits them.

The course has undergone a number of modifications during its time, but many of the original features remain. As Frank Rennie, Prestwick's professional since 1962 and only the seventh in the Club's history to hold that position, puts it: "It's the way traditional golf used to be played, through the humps and hollows along the links. It's all natural terrain and it hasn't changed very much. Half a dozen greens go back to Old Tom Morris's time. The fairways are narrow, the rough very heavy, and the

Opposite: The Smoke Room (detail).

Ian Lochhead, a younger member, with silver tankard.

Top: *J. M. H. (Michael) Scott, former captain.*
Center: *A. R. (Richard) Cole-Hamilton, former captain and chairman of the R&A's General Committee, in the Card Room.*
Above: *Dr. A. D. (Percy) Walker, former captain.*

Following pages: *Prestwick sleeps.*

Top: *Through the rough.* Above: *Advance guard of the Prestwick "eightsome".*
Opposite: *Searching for a ball near the 10th tee.*

greens small and undulating. The wind, of course, plays a big part. And then we've got the famous loop, which is the last 4 holes, a great test of golf that can swing matches round."

A notable feature of Prestwick's golf these days is the continued extensive use of caddies, a threatened species in so many parts of Britain and Ireland. The Club, its staff believe, employs and uses more caddies, on a regular basis, than any other club in Scotland. There is a hard-core of thirty to forty caddies which expands to seventy or more during the summer season. Support of the membership means that a relatively large number of caddies can work all year round. There is no more heartening sight than to see a Prestwick "eightsome", with every player using a caddie, cresting the Himalayas or some other tract of mountainous terrain, looking like a marauding band of Scottish reivers.

Prestwick's membership, for many years, remained true to its patrician origins. Its members were from the landed gentry, not all of whom played golf. By the time Michael Scott, a former Captain, joined in 1950, there was no doubt about the seriousness of the golf, but the membership was elderly, conservative and small. "They simply did not elect new members for a long time, and it was a club of very few people," Scott says. "My abiding memory of when I joined was that I was just about the only member under thirty years old."

But Prestwick's great tradition of inclusion, once you were within its portals, was firmly in place. "I remember quite clearly standing at the window in the Smoke Room," says Michael Scott. "I didn't think I was going to get a game because there was no one to play with. Then Charlie MacAndrew, deputy Speaker of the House of Commons, who obviously had a game arranged, came up and said: 'Have you got a game, young Scott?' 'No sir, I haven't,' I replied. 'Join us,' he said."

Richard Cole-Hamilton, another former Captain and, until recently, Chairman of the R&A's General Committee, agrees that Prestwick had an elitist image in the past. "When the ground was too hard for Lord Eglinton and his friends to chase the fox, they'd come down here and play a round of golf." The Club atmosphere in the old days, he recalls, could be quite intimidating for new members. "There was one young fellow who, when he walked past the big window of the Smoke Room, used to go down on his hands and knees so that he couldn't be seen. The professional caught him doing it and told him to stand up. 'One day,' he said, 'you'll be Captain.' And he was."

Three classic tales of the old Prestwick, all curiously involving majors, say it all. One day, the elderly Major Neilson was sitting in a big armchair in the corner of the Smoke Room, all alone, when a young member called Morty Dykes, who later won the Scottish Amateur Championship, came in. Dykes went up to him and said brightly: "Isn't it a beautiful morning, sir?" The major, his eyes still on his newspaper, reached up and pressed the bell above his head. The steward came out from behind the bar. "Steward," said Neilson, "there's a young man here who would like to discuss the weather. Will you accommodate him?"

Percy Walker, a retired doctor, remembers a Club dinner in the early 1950s during which the Captain turned to him and said that Major Galloway, who

Top: *The Smoke Room: end of the day.*
Above left: *Dining-room detail.*
Above right: *Changing-room detail.*

happened to be Percy Walker's patient, needed his doctor's attention. "He had slipped under the table during dinner and the Captain said to me, 'Don't just sit there, go and attend to your patient.' I got under the table and found the major lying there. I looked at him, came back up, and the Captain said, 'Well, what's wrong with the major?' I said, 'He's drunk, sir.' At which point a voice came up from below: 'And you, sir, are fired!'"

Percy Walker's other story brings us back to Major Neilson. "One day the Secretary (yet another major) told me to go and attend to Major Neilson because he had gone to relieve himself and fallen flat on his face in the lavatory. I bent down and took his pulse. He looked up at me with his very beady eyes and, from his rigidly horizontal position, said: 'Unhand me, sir. If I require medical assistance I shall summon my own practitioner.'"

The 1970s saw significant change at Prestwick. This was stimulated by a seriously adverse report by the fire authorities which necessitated a major building operation on the structure of the clubhouse. The estimated cost of this work far exceeded the expectations of the members and urgent steps were necessary to raise the required funds. The management of the Club's activities acquired a more professional approach. Debentures were issued, gifts were received from members old and new and most importantly, the Club's attractions were published to visiting golfers. This soon brought in the much-needed money.

"We reached out to America and the whole golfing world," says Percy Walker, who was Captain in 1976. "People started pouring in. Visitors' green fees continue to make a sizeable contribution to the now considerable annual expenditure on the upkeep of the clubhouse and the course. In some magical way the visitors all seem to absorb the spirit of the place."

Prestwick plays matches against and has many members in common with the other two senior Scottish golf clubs, the R&A and Muirfield. Like The Royal County Down Golf Club across the Irish Sea, Prestwick has a two-sided, Janus quality. During the week, especially from April to October, the visitors flood in and there is hardly a member in sight. But at weekends, notably Saturdays, the process is reversed. The visitors disappear and the members reclaim their Club. Foursomes is the most popular game, and while spring and autumn meetings and certain Club challenge trophies witness plenty of keen and competitive golf, the game is usually played for its intrinsic enjoyment and good companionship, not for greater personal glory.

Prestwick has four annual, highly popular black-tie dinner matches, in the manner of the Match Club further south, where foursomes are made up by the Recorder, announced during dinner, and then opened up to bets after dinner over port, kummel and cigars.

Prestwick's playing core is about 200 members out of a total of 300. Saturday is the big members' day, built around the famous lunch. Sunday sees much less activity, though members often play with their wives on that day. (There is no ladies' section at Prestwick, but there are facilities for lady visitors playing with members.) When the infrequent vacancies for new members occur, these are filled in equal proportions by sons of members and those with no connection to the Club, in order to balance the old and new blood.

Prestwick, however, does seem to have succeeded in lowering the average age of its membership. One of a vibrant group of younger members is Ian Lochhead, whose father is a member and who is in his mid-thirties. He is both an active golfer and, until recently, a member of the Club's eight-man committee. "What's special about this place," he says, "is the camaraderie among the members. Everybody is extremely friendly. You walk into the Smoke Room or dining-room and you are received immediately, regardless of your generation. The only thing that seems to upset people here is slow play. Bad golfers who are fast players are actually highly admired."

Prestwick's railway, which forms such a formidable hazard along the right-hand boundary of the 1st hole, is a great boon to its members. The run from Glasgow, where many of the members live and work, takes about an hour and avoids the physical danger of the roads and the severe penalties of the drink-driving laws. Some of the younger members have established a tradition of coming down together on the train for the Club's Christmas lunch, well-prepared with bottles of champagne and smoked salmon sandwiches.

Prestwick's camaraderie, so evident at the Saturday lunch table, became clear to Murray McCracken, a much-travelled golfer, when he was first invited to Prestwick. "The odd thing is that I already felt I was a member when I was still a guest," he says. "By the time I had paid a few visits, I was hooked."

A visit to the Smoke Room reinforces the point about friendliness and fun. Members are drinking their beer out of elegant silver-plated tankards donated to the Club by devotees over the years. There is much coming-and-going and frequent bursts of laughter. The clarity and euphony of the English language as spoken by educated Scots is a joy to the ear. There are Glasgow bankers, industrialists, lawyers, accountants, Ayrshire farmers, and a few local doctors. Ages span half a century, from thirty to eighty.

"Will you have another whisky before lunch?" asks one member of another.

"Certainly I will."

"Would you like a drop of water with it?"

"Only if there's room."

Someone is explaining, tongue-in-cheek, the meaning of the colours of the Club tie. "The green is for the course," he says, "the red is for port, and the white for kummel." (Members claim that the Club accounts for a third of Scotland's annual consumption of kummel, and they may well be right.)

Two younger members are discussing the peculiarities of the course, and in particular the 1st hole, where a good start is so important. Bernard Darwin's love of holes having names is mentioned. "Well, we have a new name for a feature on the 1st hole," says one young member. "You see that wee hillock over there, not far from the hole. We call that the Nipple. Reach that and things are looking good."

"I'm not sure the great Bernardo would approve of that," says his companion.

"He might not favour the phrase," rejoins the other, "but I'm sure he'd be delighted with the principle."

Kummel: The Putting Mixture

Opposite: *Wolfschmidt kummel.*
Top left: *Gin and tonic.*
Top right: *Whisky at the R&A.*
Center left: *A pint of bitter.*
Center right: *Pimms.*
Bottom: *Bar steward at Swinley Forest.*

"On Saturday, the temperature couldn't have been below thirty degrees, but a bitter east wind was blowing, and it felt like fifteen — definitely a four-kummel day." So wrote Herbert Warren Wind reporting for *The New Yorker* on the President's Putter at the Rye links in the early 1970s.

"I would always have a little kummel on the rocks before going out," says Tom Harvey, a former Captain of the R&A and the Royal West Norfolk Golf Club. "We call it putting mixture, and a great deal of mixed putting goes on after it."

The drinking of kummel (pronounced "kimmel"), a colourless, sweetish caraway-flavoured liqueur, in Britain's traditional golf clubs — the Irish have never taken to it — is a deeply engrained custom whose origins are lost in the mists of time. No Members Bar is complete without its bottle of Wolfschmidt or Metzendorff kummel. Members take it after lunch or dinner, neat, or with ice or water. Golfers bent on a competitive post-prandial round are sometimes said to rub a little of the sticky elixir on their palms in order to achieve a firmer grip on their putters. Whether this makes any difference to their game is debatable but it may help, at least at a psychological level, to compensate for the disorienting effect the alcoholic content (38 proof) of the liqueur may have on their reflexes.

Kümmel is German for caraway, the herb that gives the drink its distinctive, anise-style flavour. The liqueur probably originated in Holland, then spread rapidly along the north German coast. German golfers on their first visit to a British golf club must be surprised by the reverence accorded to what is essentially an unremarkable drink associated with fishermen and farmers back home.

Wolfschmidt kummel, now made in England according to an old Danish recipe, is the leading brand and the one most favoured by the clubs in this book. The runner-up is Metzendorff, whose inventor was the marvellously named Baron von Blanckenhagen. Metzendorff is now made in France and distributed from London.

Prestwick Golf Club claims responsibility for a third of Scotland's annual kummel consumption, an unverifiable but possibly quite credible figure. Royal St. George's Golf Club in Sandwich stocks both brands and is reputed to be close behind Prestwick, but man for man, the Sparrows at Porthcawl are certainly in the race.

Breeder of Mighty Champions

Royal Liverpool Golf Club

It is a raw November evening with gusting rain thrashing the links at Hoylake on the Wirral Peninsula in north-western England. A night to be indoors and no better place than the comfortable clubhouse of the Royal Liverpool Golf Club. Tonight is St. Andrews Night, and some hundred members, all in dinner jackets, are milling around on the ground floor where the Club's trophies and mementos are displayed. There is much bantering and laughter; a sea of ruddy faces; palpable camaraderie; and an air of expectancy.

A Scottish piper in full regalia pumps the bag and the bitter-sweet music of the Highlands, evoking Celtic pride and lost causes, fills the room. The hubbub dies down as a covey of former Captains, splendid in their red coats with dark green collars, sweep down the main stairway and take up vantage points on the broad steps.

Then begins a ritual that looks like blind man's bluff, without a blindfold, as the incumbent Captain peers myopically around him. Members jostle each other as they push this person or that into his purview. Finally, after much horsing around, he finds the man he is looking for and lays his hand on his shoulder. The room erupts into whistles, cheers and catcalls. The crowd falls back and the Captain leads his newly chosen successor up the stairs. The former Captains fall in behind and the procession makes its way up past the portraits of John Ball, Harold Hilton, Jack Graham and Bobby Jones, on into the magnificent club room which is laid out for the most sumptuous and most private dinner of the year.

"It's a terrific occasion," says Nicko Williams, who was led up those stairs in 1987, after peeling off "a rather unpleasant mask of Father Christmas" which he had worn for the occasion. "It's just for members, no formalities and no speeches."

"It's absolutely marvellous," says another member. "Bad boys having fun."

A month or so before this dinner, the current Captain, and as many of his predecessors as possible, convene to choose the new man. "It's amazing how many turn up — the aged and the lame, they all bumble in," says Nicko Williams, "and you haven't the faintest idea of who is going to be selected."

It does not usually come to a vote; someone simply "emerges", rather in the way that the British Tory party used to pick its leaders. But a former Captain remembers it being different on one occasion. "It had come down to two worthy candidates when one of our more elderly members, who was absolutely rat-eyed, awash with drink, said he'd had enough of this, and put one of them up, thus forcing a show of hands. This fellow then proceeded to vote against his own candidate, who failed to get in by one vote."

"Traditional but unstuffy," says Group Captain Christopher Moore, the Club's Secretary, when asked to sum up Royal Liverpool. There is no doubt about the tradition, for this Club's extraordinary past weaves a golden thread through the history of English golf. In May 1869 a meeting took place in the old Royal Hotel on the edge of "the Warren", a large rabbit-infested expanse of land bounded by the sandy dunes along the estuary of the river Dee. James Muir Dowie, a Scottish businessman from Liverpool, and Robert Chambers, his father-in-law, were the prime leaders behind the new golf Club. A month later the Liverpool Golf Club was officially formed, with Dowie as its Captain. George Morris, a brother of old Tom Morris of St. Andrews, was invited to lay out the course and his son, Jack, came down from Scotland to be the Club's first professional, and remained at Hoylake for over sixty years. The Club's affairs were run from the Royal Hotel until a clubhouse was built in 1896.

For the first seven years of the Club's existence, members shared the Warren with the horses and the racing fraternity of the Liverpool Hunt Club, which had its racecourse there. The only reminders of that shared era are two ornamental pineapples, formerly on the paddock gates, now on the putting green posts, and the old saddling bell which hangs in the clubhouse and summons members to Club dinners.

In time more land was leased, the original 9-hole course expanded to 12 and then to its full complement of 18, and a large and dignified clubhouse built. In 1872 the Club received its royal title from HRH the Duke of Connaught. And, in 1885, the Royal Liverpool Golf Club's long history of major events began with the first ever Amateur Championship.

Over the years, Hoylake, as the Club is often called, has accumulated a number of other "firsts". These include the first home international between England and Scotland in 1902, the first match between Britain and the United States (forerunner of the Walker Cup) in 1921, and the first English Close Championship in 1925. Ten Open Championships have been held there and no less than sixteen Amateur Championships, not to mention countless professional, amateur, ladies', international and county matches. Further, it was here that, as Bernard Darwin noted, "the rubber-cored ball burst on the world of British Golf," during the Amateur & Open championships of 1902. Only St. Andrews has hosted more major golf championships than Royal Liverpool. In recognition of its achievements, the R&A chose it to be the venue of the Amateur Championship in the year 2000.

Hoylake would not be Hoylake were it not for its "mighty champions". The famous golfers who were in Darwin's mind when he coined that phrase in 1933 were the local trio who dominated British amateur golf for nearly thirty years: John Ball, Harold Hilton and Jack Graham.

John Ball's father was the proprietor of the Royal Hotel. Only nine years old when the Club was founded, young John saw his formative years intertwine with the develop-

Previous pages:
Looking west over the practise ground.
Opposite:
Club gold medal (1870).

Following pages:
Revetted bunker at the 11th hole, the Alps.

Top: *Past captains.*
Above left: *D. G. (David) Beazley, former captain.*
Above right: *John Behrend, former captain of the Club and the R&A, and golf author.*
Opposite: *Senior members and the Club secretary having an early drink in the Club Room.*

Following pages: *The Dee estuary at low tide.*

ment of the Club and the course. Ball has been rated the greatest amateur golfer that Britain ever produced. He won the Amateur Championship eight times over a span of twenty-four years (1888–1912), the last one when he was fifty years old. He was also the first amateur (and with Hilton and Jones one of the only three ever) to win the Open, in 1890 at Prestwick. As Bill Campbell has pointed out in Liverpool member John Behrend's biography of Ball, he beat the Scots at their own game, on their own ground.

Harold Hilton was born in Hoylake in 1869, the year Royal Liverpool was founded. Like Ball, his golfing talents were weaned, nurtured and matured on the Hoylake course. He began a remarkable career by winning the Open at Muirfield in 1892 at the age of 23. He went on to win it again in 1897, appropriately at Hoylake, the first time the Open came to the Club. He finally bagged the Amateur in 1900, after being runner-up on two previous occasions, a victory he would repeat three more times. In 1911, his *annus mirabilis*, he won the Amateur, the US Amateur and, in the Open at Royal St. George's, finished only one stroke away from tying for first.

The third member of Hoylake's heroic trinity was Jack Graham, a member of a family whose golfing history parallels that of the Club. Graham never won the Amateur or Open Championships and was thus overshadowed by Ball and Hilton. Yet Graham reached the semi-finals of the Amateur five times; played for Scotland for a decade, losing only two matches; was leading amateur at the Open on five occasions; twice won the Gold Vase at St. George's; and won twenty-five gold and fourteen silver medals in Club competitions. His exceptional talent was universally recognised, but death in action in Flanders in 1915, leading a company of the Liverpool Scottish (Camerons), tragically ended a golfing career that still held great promise.

Bobby Jones, who won the Open here in 1930, the second leg of his legendary Grand Slam, joins these three sons of Hoylake in the Club's portrait gallery.

First impressions of the golf course at Hoylake make it difficult to credit its fabled

J. M. (Michael) Marshall, *former captain and trustee of the Club.*

On the 9th fairway.

past. It appears unusually flat for a links course. Roads and houses line three sides of it, boxing it in, and a large internal out-of-bounds area, encompassing the practise area and affecting the 1st, 15th and 16th holes, raises many a golfer's distrust. But when you start walking the course, let alone playing it, its character and its beauty become evident. The course is nowhere as flat as you first imagined. It ripples and undulates, its famous "cops", or low, turf-covered walls, provide complexity and subtlety. As you proceed you begin to admire the cunning of the design and the variety of the challenge. The internal out-of-bounds areas are unique among British championship courses: Pat Ward-Thomas described playing the holes alongside those areas as "an exercise in fear".

The aesthetics of the links also grow on you as move away from the urban development at the clubhouse end and closer to the Dee estuary. By the time you are standing on the 11th tee, the hole closest to the water, you have a magnificent view of both the course and the estuary. When the tide is out, the deserted strand that sweeps out to link the shoreline with Hilbre Island looks like the first day of the Creation. This is one of the places where Turner might have erected his easel to paint those unforgettable seascapes and sunsets.

John Graham, Jack's nephew, a former Captain, and a Club trustee who died in late 1997, remembered how when the estuary froze over, he and some friends played across the ice all the way to Hilbre Island. "But weather rarely stops play," he said in an interview. "Hoylake is protected from the north and east winds, so you can play there nearly all the time."

John Behrend, a former Captain here and of the R&A, thinks it's a marvellous course: "The wind and ground conditions are always changing, setting you new problems. It is similar to the Old Course at St. Andrews although, day in day out, it is probably tougher. Here there is no hole where you can stand on the tee and think, well, this is an easy par."

"This is a links course but not a dramatic one," says John Heggarty, the Club professional for the last fifteen years. "The small undulations and lies are seldom completely flat. My favourite holes are the short ones along the estuary (9, 10, 11 and 12). They are very challenging but they also have great natural beauty and aesthetic appeal. Hoylake is a quality course which is just as severe a challenge for modern golfers as it was for those a hundred years ago."

Derek Green, the links manager, has done much to perfect the essential character of the course. But he is emphatic about "the need to maintain the course as a traditional links course. The pressure is on from televised golf, particularly American golf, that everything should be bright green and manicured. We have irrigation, but we use it sparingly to keep the course alive, not to keep it green."

Hoylake, like several of the traditional golf clubs in this book, was founded by affluent men who made their living and their reputations in a great city within manageable distance of their favourite links. With Prestwick it was Glasgow; Royal County Down, Belfast; Porthcawl, Cardiff; and Portmarnock, Dublin. Hoylake drew its inspiration and membership from the great port-city of Liverpool, on the other side of the Mersey. The early members of Royal Liverpool were wealthy cotton merchants, shipping barons, lawyers, stockbrokers and insurance men who often chose to live on the Wirral Peninsula and commute to the city.

Opposite: *The Captains Board.*

Following pages:
Low tide at Hoylake.
Lady members coming off the 10th green.

CAPTAINS.

- 1869 – J. MUIR DOWIE.
- 1870 – J. MUIR DOWIE.
- 1871 – LIEUT. COLONEL E. H. KENNARD.
- 1872 – LIEUT. COLONEL E. H. KENNARD.
- 1873 – JOHN DUN.
- 1874 – JOHN DUN.
- 1875 – WYNDHAM C. A. MILLIGAN.
- 1876 – HENRY HOULDSWORTH GRIERSON.
- 1877 – GEORGE R. WILSON.
- 1878 – LIEUT. COLONEL BRIGGS, 96TH REGT.
- 1879 – CHARLES COOK.
- 1880 – ALEXANDER BROWN.
- 1881 – FRANCIS MUIR.
- 1882 – JAMES MANSFIELD.
- 1883 – CHAS. D. BROWN.
- 1884 – JAMES CULLEN.
- 1885 – B. HALL BLYTH.
- 1886 – JOHN GRAHAM, JUNR.
- 1887 – ALEXANDER SINCLAIR.
- 1888 – ALEXANDER STEWART.
- 1889 – JAS. B. FORTUNE.
- 1890 – CHARLES HUTCHINGS.
- 1891 – H. W. HIND.
- 1892 – S. G. SINCLAIR.
- 1893 – T. LESLIE FERGUSON.
- 1894 – HORACE G. HUTCHINSON.
- 1895 – HELENUS R. ROBERTSON.
- 1896 – GEO. C. H. DUNLOP.
- 1897 – T. W. CROWTHER.
- 1898 – FINLAY DUN.

- 1951 – E. R. ORME – 1952
- 1953 – NORMAN W. ROBERTS.
- 1954 – JOHN L. POSTLETHWAITE.
- 1955 – JOHN A. GRAHAM.
- 1956 – G. GORDON BEAZLEY.
- 1957 – GORDON F. WILLIAMSON.
- 1958 – J. D. W. RENISON.
- 1960 – J. MICHAEL MARSHALL.
- 1961 – E. BIRCHALL.
- 1962 – A. N. L. WARNOCK.
- 1963 – ROY H. SMITH.
- 1964 – W. T. G. GATES.
- 1965 – A. G. L. LOWE.
- 1966 – W. STANLEY HULME.
- 1967 – MALCOLM H. WILLIAMS.
- 1968 – J. C. LAWRIE.
- 1969 – RT. HON. SELWYN LLOYD. C.H. M.P.
- 1970 – DAVID SHONE.
- 1971 – ALAN S. BOOTH.
- 1972 – A. H. T. CROSTHWAITE.
- 1973 – T. DRAPER WILLIAMS.
- 1974 – JOHN R. TURNER.
- 1975 – V. E. SANGSTER.
- 1976 – JOHN BEHREND.
- 1977 – D. STAVELEY TAYLOR.
- 1978 – T. G. LEIGHTON.
- 1979 – L. BRIGGS.
- 1980 – JOHN A. BROCKLEHURST.
- 1981 – ANTHONY W. SHONE.
- 1982 – ROGER T. ROBINSON.
- 1983 – JOHN REES ROBERTS.
- 1984 – D. H. S. PAIN.

- 1899 – W. S. PATTERSON.
- 1900 – C. R. COX, JUNR.
- 1901 – EDWARD EVANS JUNR.
- 1902 – A. G. RANKINE.
- 1903 – FRANK HOLROYD.
- 1904 – GEORGE PILKINGTON.
- 1905 – H. C. R. SIEVWRIGHT.
- 1906 – PETER BROWN.
- 1907 – A. M. PATERSON.
- 1908 – G. E. GODWIN.
- 1909 – A. G. LYSTER.
- 1910 – W. B. STODDART.
- 1911 – E. RAMSAY MOODIE.
- 1912 – E. A. BEAZLEY.
- 1913 – E. V. CROOKS.
- 1914 – 1919 – J. H. CLAYTON.
- 1920 – C. H. McDIARMID.
- 1921 – GERSHOM STEWART, M.P.
- 1922 – EDWARD B. ORME.
- 1923 – J. P. BROCKLEBANK.
- 1924 – ALLAN J. GRAHAM.
- 1925 – W. E. MOUNSEY.
- 1926 – JAMES BAXTER.
- 1927 – A. KENTISH BARNES.
- 1928 – STUART DOWNS.
- 1929 – KENNETH STOKER.
- 1930 – J. G. B. BEAZLEY.
- 1931 – FRANK BROCKLEHURST.
- 1932 – P. W.

- 1985 – JOHN H. SPENCE.
- 1986 – KEITH V. DODMAN.
- 1987 – J. A. COLVIN.
- 1988 – N. C. WILLIAMS.
- 1989 – T. J. MARSHALL.
- 1990 – L. M. WHITE.
- 1991 – F. D. M. LOWRY.
- 1992 – G. A. MAXWELL.
- 1993 – DAVID G. BEAZLEY.
- 1994 – J. D. W. MAXWELL.
- 1995 – N. A. WAINWRIGHT.
- 1996 – PETER L. CANEVALI.
- 1997 – ANDREW W. RENISON.

For many years the style of the Club faithfully reflected this mixture. John Graham, who joined Hoylake in 1933, recalled that "it was very much upstairs, downstairs. All my friends went to public schools. You never dreamed of calling a person who was, say, ten years older than you, anything else except 'Sir'".

And the Club atmosphere? "Well, it was *boozy*, to say the least. Our best golfer in those days, Norman Fogg, couldn't play unless he'd had what he called his 'heart-starter' (a large brandy) before he went out to play in the mornings. He'd have half a dozen gin and bitters at lunch time, followed by a couple of glasses of port and some kummel, to help his putting. He'd go out in the afternoon, semi-rolling, and his opponents used to think they could take him to the cleaners. So, they'd treble up the bet and, of course, he'd win every single time."

Another Club character was Guy Farrar, who wrote the first Club history in 1933, and later went on to become an autocratic but much-loved Secretary. They tell of him walking home one night across the golf course and almost falling over a courting couple in *flagrante delicto*. Farrar went up to the man and tapped him on the shoulder: "Look here, my man," he said. "You can't do that here." The fellow raised himself up and said: "Why not?" "Well, for one thing," Guy Farrar replied, "you're not a member."

Michael Marshall, a Club trustee and former Captain whose father and son were also Hoylake Captains, joined in the 1930s and recalls the heavy drinking, big spending, larger-than-life characters and strong opinions. "They were more peppery in those days," he says with a smile. "They told you in no uncertain fashion what they thought of you, or anybody else, if you crossed their path. It's quite different today."

Royal Liverpool, in common with other venerable golf clubs in Britain and Ireland, has had its share of misfortunes. The post-war decline of Liverpool had its effect, and by the early-1970s, this grand old Club, like Prestwick and others, was experiencing hard times. The committees of the day had no long-term strategy in place, the course was in poor condition, and the clubhouse showed alarming signs of structural fatigue. One day a member who was playing snooker was about to pot a long black for what he called "a famous victory on the green baize", when part of the clubhouse roof caved in with a resounding crash. His cue ball, instead of the black, shot into the centre pocket.

Although some pretty desperate measures had to be adopted — such as increasing the membership and recruiting new members from local golf clubs — the Club gradually got its act together. A Chairman of Council, with a three-year tenure, was appointed, leaving the Captain to perform the representational duties. In 1984 Derek Green arrived as links manager and launched a programme of major improvements to the course, including a new watering system for which the R&A provided substantial funds. More recently, an equally large investment has gone into modernising and refurbishing the clubhouse. Money was raised from the membership, entrance and subscription fees were increased and, fortuitously, a sizeable tax refund came in from the government.

"We are ready for the twenty-first century," says Chris Moore. "The clubhouse is now up to the standard of the golf course, both on a grand scale perhaps, but it's still very definitely a club, not a hotel. It has warmth and dignity."

Royal Liverpool has 360 full playing members who live within fifty miles of the Club, about 200 of whom are active. There is a dynamic junior section (twelve to eighteen

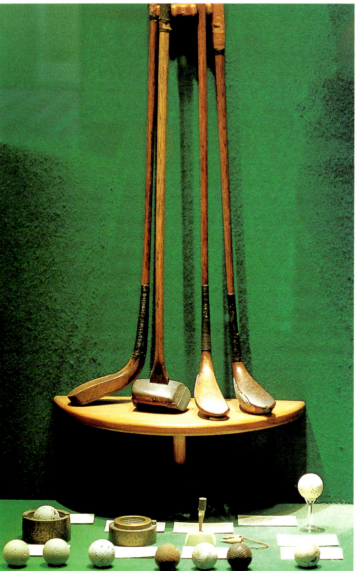

Top: *Famous portraits of Bobby Jones (left) and Harold Hilton.*
Above: *Golfing memorabilia in the hall display.*

Following pages: *The course from the Club Room window.*

years of age), forty overseas members, and 100 ladies who run their own affairs in a separate club (they have a modest but comfortable wing of the clubhouse). Hoylake leaves a small amount of room in the membership for outstanding candidates to enter relatively quickly. Golfing prowess is highly rated but so is clubability and a sense of fun, for Hoylake, without wearing its heart on its sleeve, takes its great twin traditions of golf and male companionship seriously.

There are groups associated with the Club such as the Hittites, which embraces most of the Club's hierarchy, including its three trustees ("grandees", a younger member irreverently calls them), as well as outsiders, and is sometimes referred to as "a golfing society that drinks". In contrast, there is another group called the Acers, which is more often characterised as "a drinking society that occasionally plays golf," and whose Captain is called the Trump.

Hoylake is addressing the problem of an ageing membership partly through its active junior section, and partly by opening its doors to good, young, socially acceptable golfers who come into the area. One of the latter is Graham Brown, a Scot who plays off scratch, a county player and president of the Cheshire Union of Golf Clubs. In his early forties, he has been a member for almost twenty years, is active on Club committees, and can do an enviable impression of Seve Ballesteros talking about the Ryder Cup and other weighty matters.

"It's a very friendly Club," Graham Brown says. "But it's a big Club with a large playing membership. It's not like the Prestwicks of this world. Liverpool is much closer to us than Glasgow is to Prestwick. We're only twenty minutes away from the city centre and are therefore more like a suburban club. People living in London would give an arm and a leg to have a place like this so close to them."

Hoylake's ties with the local community are maintained through the Village Play Club, a group of thirty-five local tradesmen who live within five miles of the old parish boundary. They pay no dues but, in return for using the course, they work on it, doing divoting, mending fences, painting sheds and carrying out security patrols. Their president is traditionally one of Hoylake's past Captains. They have their own pavilion, but they hold their annual general meeting and annual dinner in the clubhouse and play regular matches against the Club and the ladies' section.

The improvements to the clubhouse have enhanced the dignity of the red-bricked late-Victorian edifice without diminishing its human warmth. The inner hall, where the members gather on St. Andrews' Night, could grace any golf museum with its trophies, clubs, and golfing memorabilia. On the same level is the Mixed Lounge and the all-male Locker Bar which together share a fine view of the course. Upstairs embraces the Card Room, the Billiard Room, the Dining Room and the physical heart and the spiritual centre of Royal Liverpool, the Club Room. All the major dinners are held in the Club Room, which is a large, lofty-ceilinged, oak-panelled room generously endowed with windows on the golf course side. Over the door is the Captains Board and around the walls is a gallery of slightly camp, hand-painted photographic portraits of the past Captains, all in their red jackets. At each end of the room are fireplaces with unadorned marble mantles commemorating Club members who fell in the two world wars.

It would be easy to be overawed in such a setting but, as one former Captain put it, "the members of Hoylake are, with few exceptions, genial, generous and not conspicuously well-behaved." A sampling of the Club membership, albeit unscientific, reveals the essential truth of this statement. Drop into the Club Room on a mid-week lunch-time and you might find a group of elderly members, the Wednesday Boys, having a drink and reminiscing. One of them lives in a flat overlooking the 16th green and, when the time comes, wants his ashes to be scattered over the practise ground. "It'll be the only time that I will have been there," he says with a chuckle.

Old Leslie Edwards, sports editor for the *Liverpool Daily Post and Echo* for many years and a walking archive of golf lore, sits by the fire sipping his claret, the bottle warming on the hearth. Jos Armitage, who drew cartoons for *Punch* for years under the pen-name Ionicus, gets off his bike and comes into the clubhouse. As a child, he saw Walter Hagen win the Open at Hoylake in 1924 and remembers the new champion's wife running across the 18th green to kiss him. (Armitage has since died). And later in the day, some of the harder drinking, livelier members gather in the Locker Bar.

One of them has just peeled off the black eye patch he wears when playing and is ordering drinks at the bar. His golfing partner explains that this fellow adores country sports and damaged his eye in a shooting accident. "But it doesn't stop him shooting. He's got to kill something every day."

The sense of enjoyment that Hoylake's members take in each other's company, on and off the golf course, is surely the defining criterion of this and the other great clubs in this book. The only sad note is the current inability of the Club to stage another Open Championship. Ironically, this has nothing to do with the links, which remain a first class championship challenge, but the infrastructure that a club now requires for such a tournament. Although road access and hotel accommodation have improved since the Club's last Open in 1967, Hoylake lacks the immediate space for car parks and the tented village. At present there seems to be no way round this unless, as is unlikely, the R&A were to curtail the number of spectators and the amount of paraphernalia that has become a standard part of the Open. Nevertheless, it remains an ambition for many in the Club.

Meanwhile, Club members believe strongly in sharing their good fortune with the greater world of golf. Visitors, whether in societies or as individuals, are given a warm welcome so that they can play in the footsteps of John Ball, Harold Hilton, Jack Graham and Bobby Jones and share the exuberant spirit of the membership in the clubhouse. For this is a Club that lives comfortably with its history, yet believes it still has a future, and will surely have no difficulty in living up to its motto, "Far and Sure".

Historical Note on an Historic Club. Rumour has it that "the laying-on-of-hands" ceremony for the new Captain at the St. Andrews Dinner may have less to do with history than most members assume, and more to do with the fertile minds of John Graham and his close friend John Barratt, known, with good reason, as the "Duke of Angostura". Until about fifteen years ago, the name of the new Captain was simply put up on the Club notice-board and that was that. Word then filtered out, according to John Graham, of an ancient custom that had fallen into disuse: that in the dim, distant past the Club used to make the announcement in a much more colourful and joyful way. Hoylake being Hoylake, the members needed no further prodding and the current ritual was quickly adopted.

The Royal St. George's Golf Club

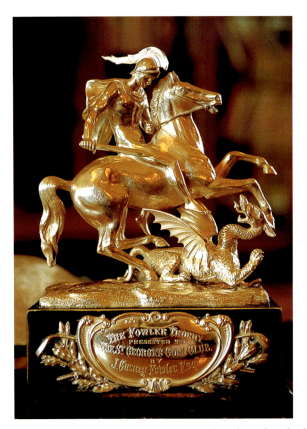

Most golfers, on arriving at a new golf club, want to get out onto the course without delay. At the Royal St. George's Golf Club in Sandwich, however, it is worth tightening the belt of expectation and first stopping at St. Clement's church in the centre of this old Kentish town. Climb the spiral stair of the 900-year-old Norman tower and gaze around you. From there you will behold a remarkably unchanged historic English borough, one of the five ancient Cinque Ports, and a marvellous panorama of the largest links course in England. You will also do homage to the man who stood exactly where you stand, over a century ago, stared northwards and saw an astonishing vista of windswept, salt and floral-scented dunes which, apart from a cluster of coastguard houses, showed no signs of human habitation.

William Laidlaw Purves, a Scottish doctor, surgeon and golfer who played off scratch, came down to Sandwich in the autumn of 1885 with his brother, a keen archaeologist, who wanted to see the place where the Emperor Claudius landed in Britain in 43 AD. The top of the church tower was chosen for an initial reconnaissance. But once William Purves saw the vast expanse of rolling dunes to the north of the town, bordered by the river Stour and the English Channel, Roman Britain was forgotten. He had seen the promised land and, as a Scottish golfer, there was only one thing to be done with it.

With typical Victorian vigour and despatch, Dr. Purves set about leasing the land from the Earl of Guilford, recruiting members, and building a golf course. On a boundary of the land was a farmhouse which became the nucleus of the clubhouse. Two Scottish golfing friends, Henry Lamb and William Robert Anderson, joined forces with the doctor and within eighteen months of the siting from St. Clement's, the new Club was taking shape. An inaugural meeting was held at the Metropole Hotel in London in May 1887, followed, a week later, by the first golf meeting of the Club on the links of Sandwich. At this point, 130 members had signed up, the clubhouse was "very comfortably arranged", and lunches and snacks were sent along from The Bell Hotel in Sandwich. Members rapidly became attached to their new Club and one of them, Tommy Mills, was so taken with the magic of the place that, after booking in for a weekend at The Bell in 1888, he remained there until his death 44 years later. The doctor-founder of the Club was reported to be so pleased with his creation that he named it after England's patron saint. St. George's Golf Club, he was convinced, would become the English equivalent of St. Andrews.

His confidence was not misplaced. In 1894, a mere seven years after its foundation, St. George's hosted the Open Championship, the first time it had ever been played outside Scotland. John H. Taylor won that time. Over the years the course has been modified to keep pace with the game and the Open repeatedly returned to Sandwich. Virtually every other kind of tournament—professional and amateur—has been played over these expansive and testing dunes. The British PGA Championship was there on five separate occasions between 1975 and 1983; the Walker Cup in 1930 (won by the US captained by Bobby Jones in the year of his Grand Slam) and 1967; the Curtis Cup in 1988; the Amateur Championship no fewer than twelve times; and the English Amateur Championship on five occasions.

A reward for the challenging magnificence of the new Club's golf links came quickly in the form of royal patronage. In 1902 King Edward VII granted the Club the right to call itself The Royal St. George's Golf Club and, later, his oldest son, the Prince of Wales (later Edward VIII) accepted the captaincy, while the prince's younger brother, the Duke of York (later King George VI) became an honorary member. In its first half century, the Club's presidency had a distinctly aristocratic flavour. The Earl of Granville was followed by Lord Northbourne who was followed by the Earl of Guilford, then by Sir Eric Hambro, who was succeeded by the Marquess of Linlithgow.

St. George's "golfing royalty" is no less impressive. Sixteen members over the years have played for the Walker Cup team and a number have been captains including, in the post-war years, G. A. Hill, P. B. ("Laddie") Lucas, Gerald Micklem and Michael Bonallack. Bernard Darwin, an aristocrat of the pen, later became president of St. George's. "No course is closer to the golfing heart of England than Royal St. George's of Sandwich," wrote Pat Ward-Thomas in 1976.

St. George's Club history is entitled *A Course for Heroes*. A combination of rolling fairways, holes constantly changing direction, strategically placed and often towering bunkers, and strong but varying winds have made St. George's (or simply Sandwich, as it is often called) one of the severest tests of golf in the British Isles. The proof of the pudding is that only two winners of the many Open Championships played on the course, Bill Rogers in 1981 and Greg Norman in 1993, have managed to be under par after the 72 holes.

"They say one test of a great course," writes Lord Deedes in the Club history, "is being able to remember every hole after the first round you play there. That feat is possible at St. George's, because no two holes are remotely alike."

"Every hole here is a potential bogey or double bogey," believes Andrew Brooks, the Club professional and former Walker Cup player. "The fairways here are very undulating and the difficulty is hitting a long to medium iron with the ball above, or below, your feet on a down slope or on an up slope. At St. George's you have to drive it long and straight, you have to play your irons better than you normally do, and you

Previous pages:
The 1st tee at Royal St. George's.
Opposite:
The Fowler Trophy, now called the Summer Cup.

Following pages:
Driving off from the 1st tee – members, caddies and dog. Lining up a putt, 6th green, the Maiden.

must putt well. There's no escape on this golf course.

"Among the more challenging holes on this demanding course are the 1st hole, 440 yards long, an awesome start that looks as if it's a straight tee shot but in fact is a slight dogleg that lulls you into driving into the right rough when you think you've hit it dead centre. St. George's is still said to be full of blind shots, but now a blind shot usually results only from a poor drive. The 4th hole has a huge bunker, supported by railway sleepers at the top of a hill. (To a military eye this monstrous bunker would not look out of place on a Marine Commando assault course.) Even if the tee shot clears this, there is still a second shot of 200 yards to a green with a deep hollow in front of it, into which a less than perfect shot may retreat off the green. The 6th hole is a beautiful par 3 called the Maiden because Dr. Purves considered the sand dune which had to be overcome to be as much a challenge as the Swiss mountain the Jungfrau.

"The 9th hole is well-bunkered and the wind here usually blows across the green. A good shot can roll up the green and catch the wrong side of the slope and run right off the green, thirty or forty feet. The finishing holes are among the strongest in golf. The 15th, a par 4 of 466 yards, needs a good drive to escape bunkers on the left and on the right. Three traps crossing the fairway short of the green make a run-up shot difficult; it's easy to take a five on it. The 16th is another challenging par 3 into the wind; the 17th, into the prevailing wind, is 425 yards. To have any chance of a level lie you need an exceptionally accurate drive, and even then, the second shot to a green with a hollow in front and five traps surrounding presents a difficult choice between a run-up or carrying the green. The 18th can be 468 yards of sheer terror, with out-of-bounds down the right, serious rough on the left, and a green so contoured as to appear to have a mind of its own as to where the shot will end up."

Andrew Brooks ends his tour with a comment on the wind. "Traditionally, a seaside course is out and in, like St. Andrews, down wind one way and the opposite coming back. St. George's goes round in two circles, constantly changing direction."

Lord Deedes, a renowned newspaper editor who as a schoolboy was a spectator at the 1930 Walker Cup match, points to two features that make the course great. The first is its "absence of artificiality", meaning that the course has retained its natural qualities, notwithstanding modifications over the years to meet the demands of modern competitive golf. The second feature is its "matchless diversity".

The links are also endowed with great beauty. So pristine, so protected is the landscape that the presence of a golf course is not immediately apparent as you approach. There are large meadows dotted with sheep, a few beleaguered trees, a church tower, and some scattered buildings — stark and simple reference points on a great rolling plain with the sea as a distant backdrop. Then the distinctive thatched-roofed beehive shelters and the white flags with the red cross of St. George (made by the caddiemaster's wife), flying from every hole, render the course instantly recognisable. On a bright summer's day, the marram grass and a host of wild flowers, including the rare lizard orchid and clove-scented broomrape, tremble in the wind. Mallard, kestrels, gulls, and skylarks cavort in the air currents above.

Opposite top: *Silver trophy detail, from the Veterans' Prize, always competed for at the Spring Meeting.*
Opposite bottom: *Sugar-encrusted red currants.*

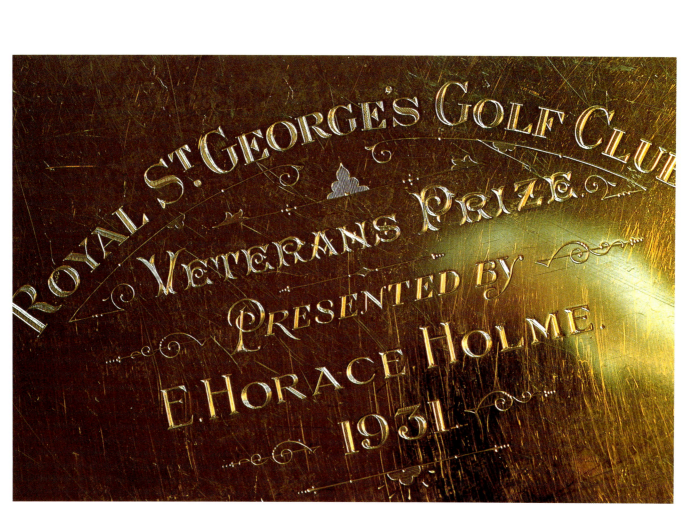

Top: M. F. (Michael) Attenborough, former captain of the Club and the R&A.
Above left: F. R. ("Bobby") Furber, former captain and Club historian.
Above right: E. W. ("Jim") Swanton, cricket and golf writer.

Above: *Club presidents' board and silver clubs with captains' balls, Smoking Room.*

Following pages: *Walking to the 7th tee.*

St. George's clubhouse matches the quality of the course. It combines the attributes of a museum, an inn, a three-star restaurant, and a very private men's club. The Club's golfing glory is artfully presented so that a visitor can absorb a good part of it while in ambulatory motion en route for the bar. The wood-panelled entrance hall displays the winners of the St. George's Grand Challenge Cup, a Club competition for amateurs with a handicap of three or less dating from 1888: the winners' names are a veritable who's who of golf including the peerless John Ball, Francis Ouimet and Jack Nicklaus. The corridor bar, still called the Smoking Room, is lined with cases of silver trophies, medals and ancient golf clubs, and with portraits of past Captains: the Earl of Winchilsea and Nottingham, for example, with his lordly mien, drooping moustache and matching check jacket, waistcoat and tie; or Lord Brabazon of Tara, PC, MC, an elegant-looking gentleman with a long cigarette-holder epitomising the Cecil Beaton look. (It comes as no surprise to learn that Lord Brabazon designed the striking Club tie in 1931.)

The Club now has a nine-bedroomed dormy house, attached to the main clubhouse, and one of the finest bills of fare found in any golf club. Sumptuous, bespoke English breakfasts (just tell the kitchen what you want and you will get it, piping hot and in abundance) are followed by a varied and imaginative lunch menu, especially on the weekends when the chef, Moira Anderson, who happens to the chief steward's wife, cooks up a storm.

The Smoking Room, with its honour boards, its leather armchairs and its fine if distant view of the course, reflects both the Club's venerable history and its intimate character. It is an elegant setting, full of history and golfing memories, where members and their guests enjoy a drink before or after a game. St. George's started as a London club and remains one. Unlike Rye down the coast, which has a homely, country *bonhomie*, St. George's presents a more polished and reserved demeanor. A St. George's member, formerly at Rye, was once asked why he had changed clubs. His careful reply was that Rye was too long a trip for him. When asked where he lived, the reply was Chile.

Michael Attenborough, a former Captain of the Club and of the R&A, and a Walker Cup player, says that the Club used to be quite "stuffy" but is far less so now. "When I became Captain, I asked the Secretary about the pitfalls ahead, and he said: 'If the course is playing well, the beef is properly cooked, and the bar prices don't go up too much, you'll have a good year.' And he was absolutely right."

"The majority of the 675 full members live in the capital," says the Secretary Gerald Watts. "Most members are from the London area. But the active membership is relatively small, probably in the range of 150 members, and more rounds of golf are played by non-members than by members."

"This is a very traditional club," continues Gerald Watts, a former prep school headmaster and sportsman of many talents. "If you are lucky enough to be a club that hosts the Open Championship then you have a degree of obligation to the big wide world of golf. We don't make any money out of the Open Championship itself, but there is quite a spin-off. Everyone wants to come and play here and if you opened up at 6 o'clock in the morning, you'd have people here then."

Opposite: *The quintessential English breakfast at St. George's.*

Following pages: *Members in the Smoking Room.*

120.

Opposite top left: *Keith Atkinson, caddiemaster.*
Opposite bottom left: *Tee box.*
Top left: *Captains' portrait gallery.*
Left: *A round begins.*
Top: *Mr. Anderson, Club steward.*
Above: *Mrs. Anderson (far right) and dining room staff.*

Following pages:
Members and guests preparing for a match.
Bunkers facing golfers driving on the 4th hole.

One result of the Club's visitor play and its sound financial footing (it owns the freehold of the course and all the surrounding meadows) is that subscriptions have been kept down and remain reasonable. But becoming a member is difficult. People with a handicap over 18, or over the age of sixty, are unlikely to make it. And even those who have passed the rigorous selection process have to wait to fill "dead men's shoes". Five or six deaths plus a few resignations a year is the normal turnover.

This suits the membership as a whole. "We've resisted virtually everything here," says a veteran member who joined over fifty years ago and whose father before him was also a member for half a century. After heated debate, a bar has replaced a steward on the end of a bell, and carpets have been changed. "And we have particularly resisted the ladies," adds the veteran.

In common with the R&A, Prestwick and Swinley Forest, St. George's does not have lady members, although wives and female friends of members may play on the course. Ironically, Dr. Purves, the founder, was a great supporter of ladies' golf and established the Ladies Golf Union, thus putting feminine golf on an official footing. Ladies' tournaments have been played at the Club as early as 1895 when the first Lady Amateur Champion, Lady Margaret Scott, played there.

Ladies' international events at Sandwich include the England–France match in 1966 and the Curtis Cup in 1988. Several wives and other relatives of St. George's members made their mark in the game in the 1930s, notably Baba, the wife of John Beck. She and he were, in turn, captains of the Curtis Cup and Walker Cup teams respectively. Patience Martin played regularly for Wales and was the wife of "Ham" Martin, an English international golfer. Later on, Linda Bayman, dubbed the "Sandwich housewife" by the popular press, played a key role in the British Curtis Cup victory in 1988.

Male precedence on the course used to be enshrined in a notice on the 1st tee that read: "Members are reminded that when playing with ladies they must at all times give way to other players on the course." And then there was the occasion when a member went out to the 1st tee one morning and saw another member, accompanied by his wife, about to tee-off. "I see you are on your own, "says the first member addressing the second. "May I join you?"

Jim Swanton, the nonagenarian cricket writer whose cane, the gift of the Kent County Cricket Club, bears the insignia "90 Not Out", says the great thing about St. George's is that there are no women. "That's to say they don't exist," he says with a twinkle in his eye. "Therefore they can play and you don't have to pay for them."

Will there ever be lady members of St. George's? "I shouldn't think so," says Brian Pope, the Club's president. "There is nothing stopping them being proposed but I don't think they would get the necessary support. Besides, it is not really a ladies' course. There are no facilities or ladies' tees. Most of the ladies around here play at Deal where there is a large section for ladies. My daughters play over there." However, lady guests have access to the dining room and to the comfortable Writing Room, which has a hatch to the bar.

St. George's, like all the traditional clubs, has had its share of characters. Bobby Furber, the Club historian and an ex-Captain, remembers the men who used to sit in the window seat next to the bar, a precinct reserved, by tradition, for Club notables. "John Beck, who won the MC at the age of eighteen and captained this Club, the R&A and two Walker Cup teams, used to sit there with his great friend, Edward Bromley-Davenport, and more often than not Colonel Charles Newman VC and the fighter ace Bob Stanford-Tuck."

At one point a brick storage room to keep the beer cool was built just outside this group's favourite window, close to where they sat. When Edward Bromley-Davenport realised it blocked the sunlight he kicked up a tremendous stink and had the offending structure removed around the corner, at his own expense. The fuss died down and Edward Bromley-Davenport was content; he could feel the sun on his back once more, as he sipped his first pink gin of the day.

Jim Swanton recalls John Beck affectionately. "He was a real character. He was like an angel most of the time and then something would blow. He used to putt croquet-style, with the putter between his legs. One day he was playing in a Moles match and wearing a deer-stalker hat on a very windy day. He had a vital putt to hole and as the ball left his club, his hat blew off and enveloped the ball completely. It took him a long time to see the funny side of that."

Bobby Furber, a spry 77-year-old who was a lawyer and remains a wine buff, a bibliophile, and an accomplished jazz pianist in the style of Fats Waller, laughs when he is told that someone resigned from St. George's because he objected to the dominance and closeness of old Etonians and former Guards officers at the Club. "It's true in that when they are in a room together they tend to congregate. Individually, however, most of them are extremely nice. I'm amazed that anybody would resign for that reason." He pauses. "Here's an Old Etonian story for you. There was a Central European fellow who came to England, became assimilated, made a fortune and played good golf for a lot of money. He had beaten one of the big American hustlers at his own club and they came down here for the re-match. Both were very twitchy. The Central European drank only milk and the American only coffee. They were delayed starting because the 1st tee was reserved for an Old Etonian golf meeting. Our friend got more and more irascible. Finally, he went up to the steward and said: 'Look, when are we going to get on the tee? And who the hell are these old Estonians anyway?'"

Ian Fleming, the creator of James Bond, an old Etonian but certainly not an Estonian of any kind, was a keen member of St. George's. He was actually Captain-designate of the Club when he died unexpectedly in 1964 during a visit to Sandwich. The marvellous gladiatorial contest on the links between Bond and Goldfinger was set at St. George's, thinly disguised for the occasion as "Royal St. Mark's." The Club professional, Albert Whiting, was metamorphosed into "Alfred Blacking".

Lord Deedes sums up the essence of St. George's in the Club history: "All recollections of St. George's grand days," he writes, "must be related to the golf course's most priceless quality. It is a great championship course. Yet it remains a course, as well I know, on which men of extremely limited ability can enjoy a wonderful round of golf. With the possible exception of Muirfield, I know of no great links course so richly endowed with that dual quality."

Club Grub

Traditional golf clubs, not surprisingly, serve traditional food. The range and ambition of the cuisine, however, vary considerably. All the clubs in this book provide simple and sustaining victuals for the hungry golfer, but a few put enough passion and effort into their tables to tempt a Michelin inspector to make an unscheduled stop.

Two clubs, Sunningdale and Royal St. George's, stand out, although Prestwick produces a marvellous Saturday lunch, and Swinley Forest excels in what a member approvingly calls "nursery food." All the clubs, it should be said, have been affected by the pressures of modern life so that soups, snacks and sandwiches have often replaced the more formal lunches of past times. And there is a growing trend, especially with the younger members who have wives and families waiting for them at home, to have a drink after their round of weekend golf and skip lunch at the club altogether.

The best way to resist that trend is to take a peek into the dining-rooms of Sunningdale or Royal St. George's just before lunch on a Saturday or a Sunday. Sunningdale's dining-room is a glorious sight, even without the food: a room full of light from the many windows and French doors that open out onto the putting green and flower-filled gardens, its polished wooden floor, snowy white table linen and sparkling glass and cutlery. By 11.30 am this scene has been transformed by the appearance of a huge and sumptuous buffet that extends the entire length of one side of the room. Salmon, king prawns, fresh tongue, mussels, lamb, pork, beef and a variety of cheeses and ten different desserts, all elegantly choreographed under the hand of Chris Osborne, the head chef, who has been with the Club for twenty-six years, await the attentions of the members and their guests. The Club crest, Sunningdale's emblematic oak tree, adorns everything, right down to the egg cups and butter dishes.

The great meal at Sandwich is Sunday lunch, a lively affair where members often bring their families. The dining-room is also spacious and well-lit; over the fireplace hangs an imposing portrait of Laidlaw Purves, the founder of the Club. Listing the dishes is like reciting a litany. Starters include home-made mushroom soup, mussels, tomato salad, marinated kippers, crab-meat, prawns, salmon and garlic paté. Four white-uniformed servers are dispensing roast rib and sirloin of beef, loin of pork, honey-baked gammon, three varieties of lamb (on the rack, a saddle with a herb-flavoured crust, or marinated in mustard, garlic and honey), duck, turkey breasts and Dover sole; vegetables include roast and new potatoes, cauliflower *au gratin*, broccoli, carrots, creamed leeks, yellow and green courgettes and for those who have never left school, bubble-and-squeak.

Opposite top: *Knife and Stilton*.
Opposite bottom left: *Profiteroles*.
Opposite bottom right: *Strawberry jelly*.
Top left: *Orange tart*.
Top right: *Spotted dick with custard*.
Bottom left: *Treacle tart*.
Bottom right: *Trifle*.

As if that were not enough, head chef Moira Anderson brings down the curtain with some marvellous home-made puddings which include treacle tart (to die for); raspberry roulade; spotted dick, a suet and flour pudding anointed with golden syrup and served with custard, sugar or cream; chocolate cake; trifle; profiteroles; orange bread and butter pudding; lemon meringue pie; *crème brûlée*; and a divine berry-filled summer pudding. A selection of English and European cheeses rounds things off. Claret or white burgundy are the preferred accompaniment to all this, and port or kummel are often taken to round matters off.

Ah, Rye!

Rye Golf Club

The wind howls over the links, gusting up to forty miles an hour. Rain clouds threaten to top up the flooded marsh land where swans glide and sheep may, in the words of one poetic sports scribe, "safely swim". It is a cold day in early January, a day to be indoors. This option, however, is not even remotely considered by scores of golfers and spectators at Rye Golf Club down on England's exposed southern coast. They are scattered far and wide, battling ball, opponent and the weather, across the Club's dry and springy golf course. For today is the beginning of the most important event of the year on Rye's calendar, a time for competitive golf, catching up with old friends, a day of "serious fun". The President's Putter, "one of the very few sacred festivals of golf" according to Bernard Darwin, is in full swing.

Only the British could devise a four-day golf competition in the depths of winter. That is what the Oxford and Cambridge Golfing Society — one of the world's oldest golfing societies, which celebrated its centenary year in 1998 — did when it requested permission from Rye to use the course for that purpose in 1920. Only war (1939–46) and snow (1979) have prevented these present and former university golfers from descending en masse upon Rye every January and spending four days playing golf and celebrating their unique fraternity on the links, in the clubhouse and in the town.

This is no token competition. Today 158 players are vying for the Putter, three of which, laden with the balls of previous winners, hang in a display case in the clubhouse. Competitors' ages span more than half a century. Youth is no guarantee of success: two years ago eight of the last sixteen players in this arduous and testing match play contest were over sixty years of age. On this occasion, one of the players, Peter Gracey, is playing in his fiftieth consecutive Putter. There is one woman, Alex Boatman, competing in her first; Ted Dexter, England's former cricket captain, a past winner; and last year's Oxford University Captain, Neil Pabari, who finally triumphs in a closely fought final with Jamie Warman, a former Cambridge Blue and a three-time Putter finalist. (An Oxford or Cambridge "Blue" is a member of either university who has played for one of the teams against the other university.)

Rye and "the Society", as the Oxford & Cambridge Golfing Society is called by its members, are blood brothers. The symbolic transfusion has nourished both parties for almost eighty years. For the Club, the university golfers have brought with them excellent competitive golf, great individual players of the amateur game (including Roger Wethered and Cyril Tolley), and a group of renowned golf writers (including Bernard Darwin and Henry Longhurst); also, a healthy injection of new Club members who, having tasted the joys of the course and the hospitality of the clubhouse, just had to join. The Society found in Rye not only a loyal supporter of its activities, but the spiritual and physical home it had never had. The section of the Men's Bar known as "the Society Corner" has on display the Putters, some pictures and a memorial plaque honouring members who fell in the two world wars.

The Putter has its own legends. E. W. E. Holderness not only won the first competition in 1920 but went on to retain his title for the next three years, and then won it again in 1929. This made five victories in all, a feat only equalled by Roger Wethered. One of Wethered's successes, in the 1926 Putter, was probably unique in the history of match play golf. He was playing E. F. Storey in the final and they battled on until the 24th hole, at which point darkness overwhelmed them and they were declared joint winners. Leonard Crawley, who lived for some time in what had once been the chief coastguard's cottage at the end of the course, won the Putter four times.

The Putter has stood the test of time and the rigours of the English climate. Each year, the faithful turn up; as the older members begin to fade away, undergraduate recruits from Oxford and Cambridge struggle with the elements on the course and mingle with their elders in the clubhouse. Media coverage helps to promote and popularise the event, if for no other reason than there isn't much other competitive golf on in the middle of January. So, if you happen to look in at the Rye clubhouse during the Putter you probably will not see the ghost of Bernard Darwin (although his armchair is in the Men's Bar) but you will certainly spot some of his successors searching for the telling phrase about the dramas going on over the links and tapping it into their laptops.

Bernard Darwin has a habit of popping his head over the bunkers on many great links courses in Britain. But the Society and Rye Golf Club held a special place in his affections, and he wrote evocatively about both of them. When he put an end to Holderness's winning streak in 1924, he wrote up a marvellously tongue-in-cheek third-person account of his own victory in *The Times* under his usual anonymous byline. He also held the highest offices as Captain (fourteen years) and president (another fourteen) of the Society, and Captain of Rye twice, once in 1906 and then again, after an extraordinary leap of time which says much about his devotion to the Club, half a century later, in 1956. Towards the end of his life, Darwin wrote that "to be setting out for Rye for the great and ever-growing assembly of the President's Putter gives me a sensation different from any other that golf has to offer." Apart from his old armchair in the Men's Bar, Darwin's memory is preserved at Rye by the Bernard Darwin Youth Salver, a relatively new under-twenty-one national golf competition organised by the Club and played on the links. The salver is a magnificent silver artefact which *The Times* presented to Darwin in recognition for his work as golf correspondent for the newspaper.

Rye is one of the beautiful and lovingly preserved Cinque Ports, built on a hill over-

Previous pages:
Members advancing to the 10th tee.
Opposite:
Rye Golf Club flag.
Following pages:
Putting at the 15th.

looking the sea and marsh land, and incorporated in the fourteenth century. Rye Golf Club's beginnings as an exclusively local affair give the Club a flavour which lingers on the palate to this day. In Rye there was no wandering, homesick Scotsman driving along the coast or climbing a Norman church tower. It began rather one evening in November 1893 with a quintessential group of local notables meeting in a quintessential Rye hostelry, the George Hotel. The group included the rector of a local parish, his son (also a minister of the church); two Rye doctors, a Rye bank manager and a former mayor. The only "outsiders" were also Sussex men, three solicitors from nearby Hastings. The meeting decided unanimously to form a golf club on the Camber sand-hills, opposite Rye harbour at the mouth of the river Rother, a mile or two east of Rye town.

Like many other venerable golf clubs, Rye was created speedily — two and a half months from conception to competition — and with the help of seasoned Scottish golf veterans who were employed as professionals and greenkeepers. The Club enlisted the services of Harry Colt (who also became its inaugural Captain and then Secretary), to design the course — the first in his illustrious career as golf-course architect.

Many golf cognoscenti consider Rye the best winter golf course in the British Isles. Indeed, a number of members regard Rye as exclusively a winter course and rarely play there in summer. The game here is predominantly foursomes, including all the sixty-four Club matches, although there are regular singles competitions. Typically, play is in the morning, followed by a jovial time at the bar overlooking the course and then a hearty lunch in the bright but unadorned dining-room across the central hall. Anyone fortunate enough to be a guest at Rye will be put at ease and quickly absorbed into the bonhomie of these unpretentious Rye men.

Darwin described it as the course of "the wind and the stances" — the wind is always against you, and you are never level. "The wind can come from all directions," says Peter Marsh, the Club professional from 1962 until 1995. "The prevailing wind is south-westerly but it can be south-easterly, north-westerly or north-easterly. There have been times when, on the 11th hole, I've knocked a three wood through the green with a tail wind. But with a head wind, it took a driver, a two wood and a four iron to get there. Without a wind, this course is a pussy cat, but with one it's a tiger. It stands up and bites."

Patric Dickinson has written about the unlevel lies. "If you suffer from a lack of balance, this is not the course for you. The fairways nearly all undulate and you will find you must play a full shot from the side of a miniature down with one foot level with your nose. Going from Rye to a flatter terrain, you feel like coming ashore after a voyage — the pavement still seems to heave under your feet."

Rye's other challenge, and another claim to fame, is its superb greens. Like those at Worlington, another great winter course, they are fair, true and fast. Rye's greens owe their quality to inspired original designing, excellent soil and shingle-based drainage, and the loving care that a line of skilled greenkeepers have devoted to them, notably Frank Arnold (1929–1973) and his successor and present incumbent, Trevor Ockenden.

Another interesting aspect of the links is that the dunes run diagonally to the course with a central one that not only has four tees (the 4th, 5th, 9th and 15th), but also provides a splendid panoramic view of much of the golf course. "The dunes have been brilliantly used by the architects over the years," says Peter Gardiner-Hill, who was Captain

Top left: *Sarah Jempson, the Lady Captain.*
Top right: *P. F. (Peter) Gardiner-Hill, president of the Club and former captain of the R&A, in the Society Corner.*
Above left: *Men's Bar discussion.*
Above right: *R. C. (Rupert) Ross, former president of the Club.*

Following pages: *President's Putter gallery.*

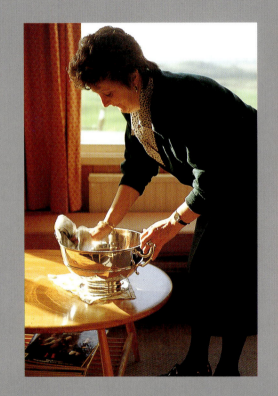

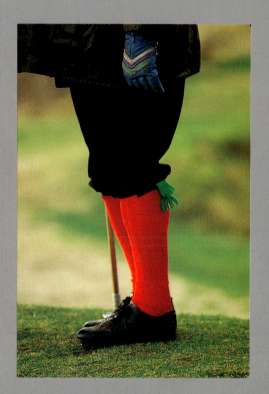

Opposite left: *Denise with Club silver.*
Opposite center: *Inscription on Club centenary gift.*
Opposite right: *Plus-twos.*
Above left: *Historic society caricatures.*
Above center: *Craft Club logo.*
Above right: *Members' favourite: buttered eggs and ham.*

Following pages: *The 18th green and clubhouse, January, 1998.*

of Rye during its centenary year and president of the Club. "Managing the course is making sure you are in the right spot for your second shot to the short par 3s, four of which are among the best in the world (2nd, 5th, 7th and 14th), and the right place to play the third shot for the par 4s. If you don't hit the greens or those spots, you are dead."

Rye is in the lucky position of having the sea as a provider of land rather than, as is so often the case on coastal courses, an eroder and eliminator. Such has been the build-up over the years that the Club has been able to construct a new 9-hole course on reclaimed land — the Jubilee Course designed by Frank Pennink and opened in 1976 — with space left over. The Jubilee Course has a different character from the Old Course; it is flatter, has a tendency to retain water and commands a less imperious view. It is nevertheless well-designed and could blossom into a fully fledged 18-hole course if the sea remains munificent.

The Club is also in the happy position of owning the links and other tracts of land that have gravel pits on them which provide a major source of income. This revenue has been critical for many decades, enabling the Club to re-build its clubhouse (which had been hit by a flying bomb in the closing stages of the war), upgrade the course and construct a reservoir. The result is that members have never been asked for extra funds and both the entrance fee and the annual subscription remain remarkably low. Another consequence of financial security is that, unlike many traditional golf clubs, Rye does not need visitors' green fees to pay its way. Suitably introduced visitors may play the course, but the numbers are few, and this suits the members and their guests perfectly.

For a club that started as a local enterprise, Rye has always had a large proportion of "country members" (currently almost half the full male membership) — that is people who live over forty-six miles from the Club and who pay a lower subscription. Thus London-based "country members" can play on a marvellous links course, about an hour and a half's drive away, for a modest amount. But Rye retains its distinctly old shoe local flavour and its London members check any reserved city ways at the door.

How hard is it to get into Rye? "The waiting list is three to four years," says Rupert Ross, Rye's dapper octogenarian former President. "We don't want our numbers to increase because of the limited capacity of the course. We're not being bloody-minded but, with about 400 active members, we've really got enough."

As people live longer and play more golf, Rye like so many other clubs, has experienced an ageing membership. There is, however, a 130-strong cadet section (one of the most popular events being the October fathers-and-sons foursomes competition), and a steady influx of youth from the Society. Rye also has an associated Artisans' Club, mainly local tradespeople who play the courses at fixed times, and an independent ladies' section consisting of 135 members, of whom fifty to sixty are regular golfers.

Sarah Jempson, the Lady Captain is, like many of her co-members, the wife of a Rye member. "Before I joined the Club in 1980 I heard that women were second-class citizens. But perhaps because I was one of the younger ones, I found this quite untrue. The men were immediately friendly." But the Men's Bar was inviolate. When Fiona McDonald, a Cambridge "Blue", was playing in the President's Putter a decade ago and was allowed in the Men's Bar as an "honorary man", a female member, who had been a very good golfer in her day, walked up the steps of the clubhouse and into the Men's Bar.

The listening captain.

Following pages: *The 7th green.*

"When it was politely suggested that she should leave, she refused, on the grounds that there was already a lady in the bar, but she left none the less."

Things are somewhat different now. During the President's Putter, when the Society is allowed the run of the Club, lady players are allowed the freedom of the Men's Bar, and the ladies' section have exclusive use of the Men's Bar three times a year, for their spring, autumn and invitation meetings. "I don't think there is any woman here who resents the separate bar, or would change anything. The ladies' section is completely self-governing and there are no hard feelings at all," says Sarah Jempson.

Rye would probably not be Rye if it did not have diversity under its roof. There are many other societies and groups, formal and informal, who play at Rye. But at the core of the Club there is a good mix of local and more distant members that includes many lawyers, farmers, former servicemen and plenty of other professional and business people.

There is also a rather special group, the Craft Club, formed on April Fool's Day, 1991, by a pair of elderly members who were stood up for a game by their equally elderly opponents. The spokesman of the miscreants later apologised profusely with the comment: "Awfully sorry, old boy, but these days I can't remember a f. . . thing." This inspired Tom McMillan and Jim Marsham to found the Craft Club (its logo was quickly bowdlerised to "Can't Remember a Flipping Thing") which, by levying a £5 one-time entrance fee on its members, has raised the astonishing sum of over £90,000 from some 17,000 members around the world for three prominent charities. The Craft Club insignia is an elephant with knots in its trunk and tail.

Apart from the Putter, Rye has not been a course of championships (its relative shortness in the championship season precludes that), but it has always attracted good golfers who often happened to be prominent in other spheres of life, an impressive group of golfing societies and a fair share of "characters". A. J. Balfour, the Tory prime minister, was an early member, keen golfer and Captain (also Captain of the R&A the year Rye was founded), as was his colonial secretary, the Honourable Alfred Lyttelton, a prodigious athlete who had played cricket and football for England; two future kings, Edward VIII and George VI, were honorary members; and Henry James, who had made Rye his English home and was elected a member of the golf club. There is no record of any golfing feats — or indeed any golfing at all — by the great American novelist; it appears he came to the clubhouse solely for the afternoon teas, which he much enjoyed.

"Rye is the home of societies," says Peter Gardiner-Hill. "For some of them it is their base, for others the place where they traditionally play their annual meeting." Some thirty golfing societies treat Rye as a regular port of call. The societies reflect the connections of Rye's past membership: the Parliamentary GS and the Bar GS links go back a long way, as do those with the golfing societies of some of Britain's leading public schools, such as Charterhouse, Rugby, Sherborne, Wellington and Winchester, who are among those who also play matches against the Club.

Like some other traditional golf clubs, Rye has had its autocratic Secretaries, gentlemen who by force of personality, helped by a mixture of complaisance and laissez-faire on the part of the Club's officers and membership, ruled the roost. One of the most authoritarian and eccentric was Brigadier Rupert Scott, DSO, who held sway from 1948 until his death in 1961. He was, and looked like, the old-style regular army officer — close-cropped hair parted down the middle, military moustache and monocle. One of Rye's members who survived a dinner at the brigadier's bachelor home where sherry and port were served in pint mugs before and after the meal, later wrote about him:

"He was six foot four square, he had been left for dead, at sixteen, in 1917, and he had survived. He was larger than life or death. On the mantelpiece in his flat was a human skull with the date on its dome in biro. A Japanese sniper had killed two of his best men. The Brigadier had gone out, tracked him down, killed him and beheaded him."

Brigadier Scott believed firmly in keeping up the old standards and any irregularity brought down a fearsome wrath on the transgressor. He was particularly incensed by slow play and used to keep his monocle trained on golfers from his office, which overlooked the 18th green. One summer evening, this same member and a friend were unwisely having a putting contest there when he heard a violent explosion. "A spare ball a yard to our left became self-propelled and suddenly ovoid. There was a bellow from the Secretary's window. There he was, iron-grey, bullet-headed, gold-rimmed monocle in maroon face laughing his head off, revolver in hand. Clearly, the Brigadier was a good shot, how good we did not wait to see as he took aim again."

The present Secretary, Lt. Colonel Chris Gilbert, is also a military man although he does not wear a monocle or keep a revolver on his desk. His brief, he says, is to keep things as they are. "If a member only comes here once every four years, the warmth and ambience of the Club should be exactly as it was when he left: the newspapers and record books in their traditional place. The staff know all their names, their quirks. It's very anachronistic here and we make our mistakes extremely slowly." How will the Club be in twenty years time? "It could well be exactly the same," says Chris Gilbert. "We believe we have achieved karma here, so why should we change."

Rye is without doubt a slightly odd place, a club where eccentricity sits comfortably with orthodoxy, conservatism with adaptability, elitism with friendliness. Members still tend to call each other by their surnames, as if they had never left their prep schools — "people come down here for a weekend and behave as if they are back at school," said one Rye veteran; on the opening day of the President's Putter, as the biting forty-mile-an-hour wind belted in from the sea, one member drove off in a short-sleeved shirt and shorts ("he has a serious over-heating problem," an onlooker explained); Rye's culinary favourite is buttered (that is, scrambled) eggs and cold ham; while most of the older golf clubs have produced history books to celebrate their centenaries, Rye couldn't wait and put out an elegant volume entitled *Rye Golf Club: The First 90 Years*, (written by Denis Vidler); and the membership is a tight, virtually hermetic world although visitors, whoever they are and from wherever they come, invariably receive a spontaneous, warm and whole-hearted welcome in its comfortable but plain clubhouse. There is no side to Rye; it is what it is.

Chris Gilbert says that when he goes to golfing dinners and introduces himself, the reaction is reflective. "People either say, 'dear old Rye', or simply, 'Ah, Rye.' And if you ask members here what they think of the Club, they'll probably start by saying, 'Ah, Rye'. . . ." It's true that it is a beginning; but it is also an end. "Ah, Rye," somehow says it all.

A Golfer's Club

Sunningdale Golf Club

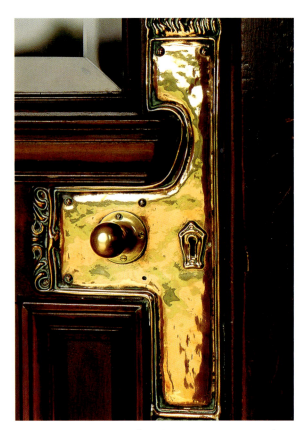

It is a lovely summer's day at Sunningdale Golf Club. The gardens around the clubhouse are in full flower and the famous oak tree, quintessential emblem of this most English of English clubs, is spreading its branches again after a severe pruning during the winter. A group of members and their wives are sitting in comfortable chairs on the verandah drinking Pimm's, talking and laughing, as Club stewards, in blue waistcoats trimmed with gold, tend to their needs. An elegant collie sits patiently at the edge of the practise putting green, its fur ruffling in the lazy summer breeze.

It is also a busy day at Sunningdale, as all weekends tend to be. More than a hundred members and their guests are out on the two courses; a contest between Sunningdale and the Match Club is in full swing; a committee meeting preoccupies the Club's movers and shakers upstairs in the Walker Cup Room; cleated golf shoes crunch purposefully on the gravel around the clubhouse; caddies with golf bags slung over their shoulders move to and fro; yet another Bentley, followed by an Aston Martin and a Ferrari, arrives in the teeming car park; and overhead a British Airways Concorde dips its aristocratic nose (surely in homage?) as it prepares to land at Heathrow Airport.

Out on the 1st tee, a group of fit-looking men in their late fifties or early sixties are discussing their matches and bets, and preparing to tee-off. First to go is Tony Biggins, Sunningdale's current Captain. Dressed all in black, with silver hair swept back, and a small cheroot in his hand, he has the bearing of a Western gunfighter. He takes a last draw on his cheroot, tosses it away, tees-up, and fires a long and perfectly-controlled drive down the fairway.

Sunningdale is the antithesis of the smaller traditional clubs such as Swinley Forest, Brancaster and Worlington. More members play here in a single day than are spotted in those clubs in a fortnight. Sunningdale zings, while a club like Swinley slumbers. It is a large club with an active membership, a club that thrives on competition, a club of talented and combative golfers, a club that opens its courses freely and proudly to the international world of tournament golf.

Situated on the same magical swath of Bagshot sand as Swinley, Wentworth and the

Berkshire, Sunningdale is the proud owner of two of the greatest heathland golf courses in the world. The Old Course was designed in 1900, when the Club was founded, by Willie Park Jr., and the New Course was built by H. S. Colt in 1922. An opinion, shared by many, is that they are probably the best *pair* of golf courses you'd encounter anywhere: this heathland golf terrain does not exist much in other countries, and is rare even in Britain.

The Old Course has a special cachet for most golfers. "It has a kind of intimacy about it," says Tony Biggins. "It looks easy but it isn't. It's very fair; there aren't any bad holes, and if you play well, it's very rewarding. But if you don't, it's very punishing, especially now that we've grown the rough up. I know many people who are not members who, if you asked them to choose one course for the rest of their lives, they'd say, 'the Old Course at Sunningdale.'"

But the New Course more than holds its own. "It's a little more open, the greens are a bit smaller and if you miss them you are penalised more than on the Old Course," Tony Biggins continues. "Strangely enough, very good players score better on the New Course than on the Old; while handicapped players normally find the New much more difficult than the Old. The New has five par 3s, and each one is better than the one before!"

While the Berkshire, Sunningdale, and Swinley clubs are all alike in having lovely wooded Bagshot sand-based courses, they differ in other ways: As a member at both Sunningdale and Swinley puts it, all the Berkshire members are gentlemen and love to play golf; all the Sunningdale members love to play golf but not all are gentlemen; and all the Swinley members are most certainly gentlemen, but they don't give a fig whether they play golf or not.

The driving force behind the founding of Sunningdale was T. A. Roberts who, with his brother, G. A. Roberts, obtained a lease from the St. John's College, Cambridge, still the freeholder of the land. The two brothers built an opulent Edwardian clubhouse with the canny calculation that, if the Club failed, it would make a fine home for one of them. H. S. Colt was its most influential figure during the first two decades of its existence, serving as Secretary, as Captain, and architect of the New Course. Royal patronage came early when the Duke of Connaught became president of the new Club in 1904 and stayed until 1914, even though the Club rules made no provision for the post.

The Club's amateur heyday was during the 1920s and 1930s, when it was intimately involved with the great competitions and golfing events of the time. Among its luminaries were Leonard Crawley, Cyril Tolley and Diana Critchley who, at the precocious age of nineteen, won the Ladies Open Championship and whose golfing prowess led to the unusual sequel of having one of the club rooms — the Mixed Lounge — named after her. During this period the Prince of Wales (later Edward VIII) and his brother, the Duke of York (later George VI), both served as Captains of the Club. And it was on the Old Course, in 1926, that Bobby Jones crafted a legendary round of golf in a qualifying round for the Open there which he went on to win. His score of 66 on the Old Course, composed of 33 for the front nine and 33 for the back (33 shots from tee to green and 33 putts), was described by Bernard Darwin as "incredible and indecent".

In more recent years, Sunningdale has hosted the Colgate Ladies European Championships (the 1970s), the Walker Cup (1987), and the Weetabix Women's British

Previous pages:
The 10th hole, Old Course, from the half-way hut.
Opposite:
Brass door-plate detail.

Following pages:
Sunningdale oak at the 18th.

Open (1997). The European Open was held on eight occasions betewen 1982 and 1992, and the winners have included such famous names as Faldo, Norman, Langer, Woosnam, Aoki, Brand, Senior, and Periero. In the year 2000, the Club's centenary, Sunningdale will stage the Solheim Cup, the women's equivalent of the Ryder Cup. Twenty members over the years have played for the Walker Cup team. Ninety Sunningdale members are members of the R&A.

A splendid annual event since 1934 has been the Sunningdale Foursomes. Played in early spring when the wind is keen and the courses are long, this knockout match-play competition is a rigorous test of an individual's ball-striking ability and self belief. Amateurs, up and coming and some less so, compete with professionals, with sometimes surprising results. Each match is over 18 holes, full handicap difference, where Professional Golfers (Men) play off +1, Amateurs (Men) off scratch, Professional Golfers (Ladies) off 2 and Lady Amateurs off 4. Everyone uses the same tees.

Current fields comprise 128 pairs entering from all over the United Kingdom, plus a smattering of entries from overseas. It is an excellent week's golf for both player and spectator and full of the amazing occurrences which the golfing gods seem to reserve for important matchplay occasions.

Sunningdale has had its fair share of mentors, great players and characters. In the post-WWII years, the man who had the most profound influence on the Club was Gerald Micklem. He lived in a lovely house on the edge of the course and helped to steer the Club through the difficult financial times that many traditional golf clubs experienced in the late 1940s, 50s and early 60s. John Whitfield, a veteran Sunningdale member and author of the history book being published for the Club's centenary, says that Micklem, after much persuasion, finally accepted the post of president not long before he died. "His condition for acquiescing was simple," says Whitfield. "'I'll accept,' he said, 'providing I don't have to do anything.'" Since Micklem's death the Club has not had a president.

Michael King, a former Walker and Ryder Cup player, who was brought into the Club as a protégé of Micklem's, remembers him well. "He was the doyen of Sunningdale," he says. "His way of handling things was to let everyone have a good scream and then do nothing. He managed to stop things — the wrong things — from happening. He sponsored the gardens," Michael King points to the floral splendour that surrounds the practise putting green. "His ashes are buried over there, among the rhododendrons."

Sunningdale was fortunate in both its caddiemaster and its professional in the postwar period. James Sheridan, a Scot, had been caddiemaster since 1911 but carried on working until 1967. Having survived the horrors of trench warfare in France in World

Opposite: Car park details.

Following pages: Storm clouds over the 5th green, New Course.
Three former captains in Members Bar.
Dining room detail.
Shot into the 17th hole, Old Course.

War I, he was nearly killed in World War II much closer to home. A German bomb landed to the right of the 18th green on the Old Course as Sheridan was about to play a shot. He saved himself by diving into a bunker on the left. The bomb crater was later turned to advantage as an additional bunker: a piece of improvisation which, most members agreed, not only greatly improved the hole but also could be regarded as German reparations for starting the war in the first place.

Derek Davies, a former Captain and trustee of the Club, recalls the caddiemaster's special contribution to Sunningdale. "If you turned up without having organised a game in advance, Jim Sheridan would say to you: 'Mr. Davies, ye're playing with Mr. Brown.' He would know that Mr. Brown was looking for a game too and that he would be all right golfingwise. And you never thought of saying to Jim Sheridan, 'I'm sorry.' You said, 'OK, fine.'"

"Sheridan was one of those superb people who would look after the caddies in the winter if there was no play," says John Boardman, another past Captain and former trustee. "He made sure they got a little money whatever happened."

Arthur Lees, a Yorkshireman and Ryder Cup player, took up the job of professional in 1949 and remained there until 1976. He made his mark as a talented teacher, a loveable human being, and a perfect foil for the high-rolling competitive low-handicap players. Like Sheridan, he became an honorary member and his portrait also hangs in the Members Bar. John Boardman recalls Lees fondly. "He was a marvellous teacher, like a doctor. You'd go to him with one facet of your game a bit off and in five minutes he'd fix it. He was also a keen gambler. You'd ask him in the bar after a game. 'Well, I tell you what,' he'd say, 'I had to shoot 62 to win. I joost won.' It was always, 'I joost won'. The gambling was fine and the people who gambled with him always wanted to come back for more. We never knew what they played for because they called them *units*." Michael King also thought highly of him. "Arthur Lees was a great golfer and gambler, liked the girls, a good fella — a proper Sunningdale chap."

Perhaps the most colourful character in recent times was an old Etonian called Julian Earl. One day he was in the bar when another member came in off the course holding a handkerchief over his face, stanching a severe nosebleed.

"Good heavens!" exclaimed Julian Earl. "What happened to you?"

"I got punched on the nose by the fellow I was playing with."

"That's awful! Did you punch him back?"

"Of course not," said the aggrieved golfer, dabbing at his nose.

"Oh," drawled Julian Earl, "if I'd known that I would have punched you years ago!"

The golfing glories of Sunningdale are enshrined on its championship, medal and team boards and its collection of silver trophies. Sunningdale's competitive character reveals itself as soon as you enter the vestibule, before crossing the threshold proper. The notice board is dominated by the Handicap List, in which you can see every member's name, with his current handicap inscribed next to it. At one glance you have the golfing hierarchy of the Club. The message is clear: at Sunningdale, the game is the thing.

Inside, a generous hallway and a broad staircase greet you. To the right, is the wood-panelled Members Bar which displays portraits in oils of famous members as well

Opposite: *James Sheridan, caddiemaster and honorary member.*

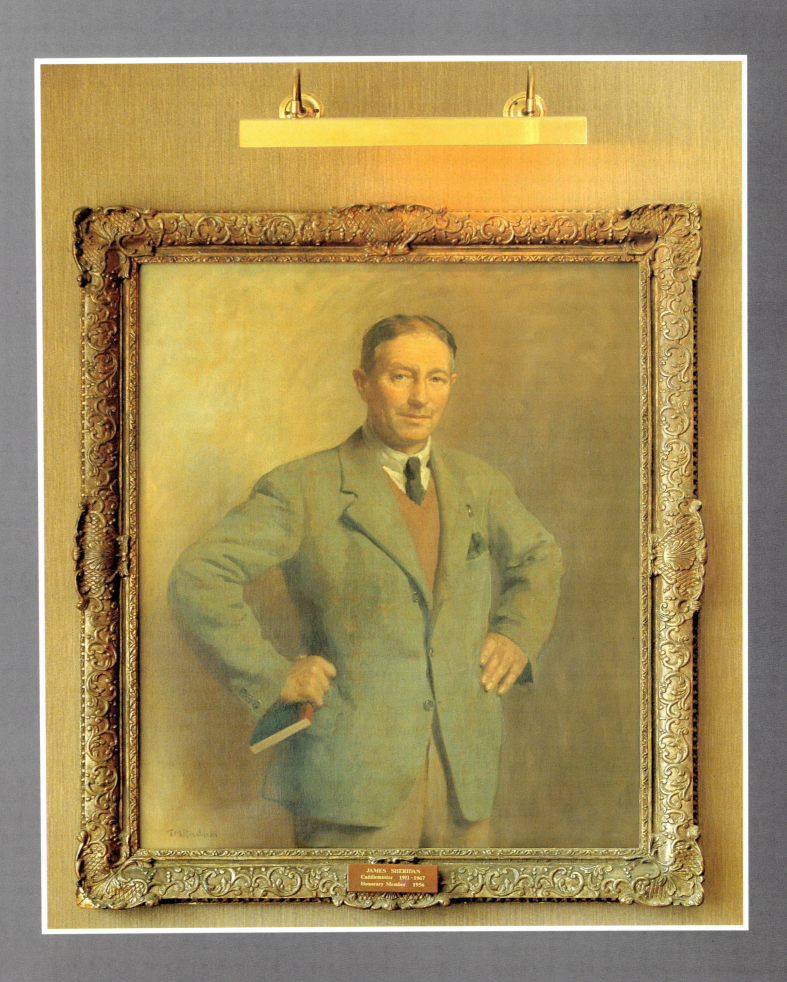

as the Club silver, in a glass cabinet laden with cups, medals and other trophies. Beyond is the members' changing-room — a modern, well-appointed complex surprisingly referred to by the American term, "locker-room". On the left of the hallway, is the Critchley Room. Here male and female visitors can have a drink, study more honour boards (as well as a portrait and a commemorative record of Bobby Jones and his famous Open victory), and feast on the marvellous vista of the practice putting green, the Sunningdale oak, the gardens and the 1st tee. At the end of the hallway is the dining-room, another light, airy space with a similar view and spectacular food.

Upstairs is the Walker Cup Room, which boasts a bar, a TV set and the Club library. Around the walls are portraits of members who played in the Walker Cup. Beyond is the Card Room, where older members play bridge with Sunningdale's own oak-crested, gold-and-blue playing cards, and the younger ones play backgammon. And then there is the Secretary's Office which, due to its elevation, has an even better view of the practise putting green, the gardens, and down the first fairway into the rhododendron-studded woods beyond. Sitting at his desk is Stewart Zuill (pronounced "Ewell"), Sunningdale's soft-voiced Scottish Secretary, overlooking the course as a captain of a great ocean liner might gaze over the bow of his ship at the distant horizon.

"Yes, there's a bit of steel in the golf at Sunningdale," he says with a smile. "The main game is four-ball, although a lot of singles are also played here. Having two courses is a great advantage. We can keep one for singles and members know that they can come here, get round in about three hours, and return to their businesses or homes."

Sunningdale is very popular with golfing societies. So much so that during the week, it sometimes seems as if the place has been invaded and occupied by the likes of Mercury Asset Management, Marks & Spencer or a fundraising organisation such as the Anthony Nolan Bone Marrow Trust. "Society and corporate days are Tuesdays, Wednesdays and Thursdays," says Stewart Zuill. "On Mondays we take visitors who come by arrangement. Fridays, Saturdays and Sundays are purely for members and their guests. We think that the present mixture between income from visitors and members' subscriptions is fair."

"We can't accommodate members during visitors' days if they come down between 2.30 pm and 3.00 pm. They have to alternate with the societies. That's a weakness, but something that most golf clubs have to deal with as more and more senior members want to play during the week."

It's hard to imagine that Sunningdale ever had hard times, but like many of Britain's other venerable golf clubs, it suffered after the Second World War. Derek Davies remembers joining the Club in 1952. "I had played a round of golf here, in a tournament called the Lucifer Trophy, and I was standing in the bar afterwards saying what a marvellous course I thought the Old Course was. A small man standing beside me said, 'Oh, you like it do you? Would you like to be a member?' he said. Just like that. He told me to hang on, disappeared for a moment, and returned with a not very large piece of paper in his hand. 'Fill in your name, rank and number,' he said. The next thing I knew I was asked for six guineas and I was a member of Sunningdale Golf Club." Derek Davies laughs. "Things are slightly different now."

Top: *A. D. H. (Tony) Biggins, former captain.*
Above left: *John Putt (left) and Nicholas Burn.* Above right: *Bruce Critchley.*

Following pages: *Sunningdale Club silver.*

A popular, uninformed image of Sunningdale is that of a very old, very stuffy, very exclusive golf club brimming with rich, flashy upper-class toffs who turn up in their fancy cars, gamble, drink and play — roughly in that order — before returning to their London mansions or country homes. A slightly more differentiated view, taking into account Sunningdale's undeniable golfing pedigree, came in the 1930s from Henry Longhurst, the well-known golf writer and broadcaster. The occasion was the introduction of the Club tie, with its distinctive diagonal blue and brown stripes. Longhurst thought its design accurately represented Sunningdale's membership: "Half of them are Blues," he said, "and the other half are shits."

The reality is rather different than either image, although some elements of both may disguise a nugget of truth. Sunningdale is certainly old, but it is far from stuffy. Beneath the hustle and bustle, the competitive glow, the weekly invasions of golfing societies, beyond the uniformed stewards and stewardesses, the gold-encrusted honour boards, and the opulence of the trophy cabinets, is a friendly, relaxed group of surprisingly eclectic golfers. The Club has a wide range of members that include the City types one would expect — merchant bankers, Lloyds brokers, lawyers, financiers and so on — but also sportsmen, actors, schoolteachers, broadcasters, publishers and others from many walks of life. Ted Dexter, the former England cricket captain; Jackie Stewart, a Formula One racing champion (and James Hunt, now dead, before him); and actor Michael Medwin are all members. Gary Lineker, the former England footballer, has recently been proposed by Michael King; "I trust he won't get a red card," his proposer says. And while Royal St. George's may boast Ian Fleming among its illustrious alumni, Sunningdale has 007's best screen exponent, Sean Connery, on its membership rolls.

"Sunningdale had a much clearer identity forty years ago," says Bruce Critchley, a former England and Walker Cup player, son of Diana, and an old Etonian. "Before and after the war, it was public school, Oxbridge, and the best names in British golf. You've still got to be a good golfer to get in and excellent golf is still played there. There is no pomposity at Sunningdale," continues Critchley. "Members are very confident people who are comfortable with themselves. You can do and be anything you want here. Nobody gives a stuff. Celebrities like Jackie Stewart and Sean Connery can be themselves and feel at ease."

When you take a look around Sunningdale's car park on a busy Saturday morning, you can be forgiven for thinking this is a fabulously rich man's club. Rolls Royces, Bentleys, Aston Martins, blood-red Ferraris, not to mention rows of Mercedes, Porsches, Jaguars and BMWs — why, there must be millions of pounds of carflesh out there.

"It's true that we do have a number of exceedingly rich members," observes a member, "but we also have — how shall I say it? — people who are not very well off. The great thing about Sunningdale is that when a member walks through the front door of the clubhouse, everybody is the same and everybody knows it. The same people do not play each other all the time. You don't have to fix a game and there are no start times here. Any day of the week, including week-ends, you can come along and no one will be left in the clubhouse if they want to play golf. We pride ourselves on this."

Club membership is pegged at 950, of which 500 are full members and form the active core of the Club. The rest consist of seventy-five ladies, seventy cadets (between the ages of twelve and eighteen) and various overseas, country and non-playing members. "The waiting list is large," says Stewart Zuill. "You cannot get in if your handicap is above fourteen but, if you have strong support and you know some of the Club members, a good candidate will make it within a couple of years." Cadets, especially if they are good golfers, have preference over outsiders. "Cadets can apply for full membership at eighteen," says Tony Biggins. "We breed our own new blood, if you like."

One of that breed is Nicholas Burn, now in his early thirties, who came up through the cadets. His father is a former Captain and his brother is a member too; all three are also members of the R&A where they like to go, as a family, for the Autumn Meeting. Nicholas Burn played for Surrey Juniors and a lot of other competitive golf before his career as an insurance broker in the City, marriage and a young family began to reduce his time on the golf course. He recently joined the Club's general committee, his first taste of administration of a Club that he was born into. He echoes Gerald Micklem's philosophy: "As little change as possible."

As custodian of two of the best heathland golf courses in the world, the Club has always felt a need to share them with outsiders, as a venue for championships and competitions, for golfing societies and corporations, and for the golfing public in general. "I think it's very important that people come and play Sunningdale," observes Nicholas Burn. "It should be shared, not restricted to a few privileged golfers."

Sunningdale has long had a reputation as a gamblers' club. During Arthur Lees' time, thousands of pounds used to change hands. And there is still a small circle of high rollers. But the majority of members seem to bet a few pounds, or perhaps just a golf ball or two, and at the end of the day not a lot of money actually changes hands.

"Sunningdale is known for gambling," says Michael King. "Everyone tells you it isn't, but they gamble here all the time. It's one of the traditions of Sunningdale. People like a punt, and normally they can afford it. And when they can't, it doesn't matter."

"There are only about thirty big punters in the entire Club," says a long-standing member. "But they tend to be larger-than-life characters and so give the Club a name for gambling. Which it rather likes!"

The fortunes of the Club have changed over the years, but in its sporting heart Sunningdale remains true to its origins. It is still essentially a London club, with well over half of members living and working there. Modern transport means that it is only forty minutes from the centre of the capital by frequent trains, or by car on a good day, and Heathrow is a mere fifteen minutes away. In the great days of leisured amateur golf, when good golfers also had private incomes, Sunningdale was a golfers' Mecca. Those days have gone, but keen and talented golfers, who also happen to be hard-working, high-achievers in the City of London and elsewhere, still gravitate to the Club.

Sunningdale's social cachet is not what commands the loyalty of the vast majority of its existing membership, or indeed attracts new members. With its long history of golfing glory, its unquenchable competitive spirit, its physical beauty, and its professional polish, Sunningdale is unlikely to change. Derek Davies, one among many of the same opinion, has no doubt that Sunningdale will always be what it has always been: "a golfer's club".

A Haven for Golfing Gentlemen

Swinley Forest Golf Club

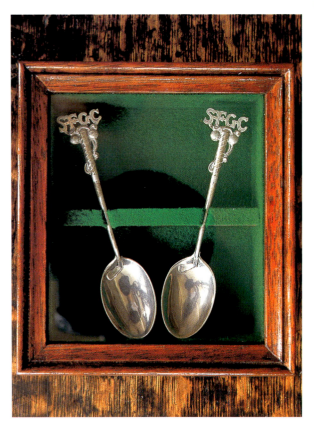

Swinley Forest Golf Club exists, it could be argued, to prove that the English are indeed an eccentric lot. For this Club is defined as much by its lacunae as by its attributes. The Club has been around for almost a century yet it has no captain, no handicaps, no monthly medal, no Club tie, no Club logo, no visible Club silver — apart from a couple of spoons — no suggestions book, and no Club history. Its professional is an amateur and, until recently, the Club had neither scorecard nor par. Mention the absence of these standard icons of a traditional golf club to a Swinley member and all you will get is a tolerant shrug and something along the lines of, "Well, that's Swinley."

To absorb the spirit of Swinley Forest, there is no better vantage point than from the depths of a well-upholstered armchair in the club room. Light floods in through leaded window-panes which afford a fine view of the course as it rolls away down through the forest. Chintz-covered sofas and chairs, a generous fireplace surmounted by an oak mantle, a grandfather clock that punctuates the quiet hours with silvery chimes, and a portrait of the Earl of Derby, who founded the Club in 1909, give the impression that you have wandered into someone's drawing-room by mistake. This is not surprising when you consider that this solid structure, with its weathered red brick and tall chimneys, was built at the zenith of the Edwardian era, when Britain was affluent and peaceful and everyone knew their place.

Characteristically, the founding of Swinley is not documented. However, the story goes that Lord Derby, a minister of the Crown in Queen Victoria's last years, went to play golf at Sunningdale one day and was held up by a slow four-ball match. As a result, he turned up late for a meeting with the Queen at Windsor Castle. On hearing the story, she chided him. "Surely, Lord Derby," she is alleged to have said, "a man in your position should have his own golf course."

The good Earl took the hint and bought a great swathe of prime heathland conveniently close to Windsor and not far from Sunningdale. He rented another chunk from the Crown and built Swinley Forest. The first members were principally his friends and cronies. Bonds were issued to the early members, with Lord Derby keeping three for himself. On the death of a bond-holder, the bond passes on to a member of the family or is bought in by the Club.

Swinley's history lies in the minds and memories of its membership. "It was always a sort of mystical place," said Jo Floyd, who was a fine golfer and a former chairman of Christie's, and who loved Swinley as well as his other two clubs, Brancaster and Worlington. The inescapable impression is that the place fell asleep many years ago and slumbered on for decades, the Rip Van Winkle of golf clubs. Membership remained small and intimate; visitors were infrequent and invariably friends of members; the clubhouse became shabbier and shabbier; and the golf course retained its original style which was, in the words of one aristocratic devotee, "a gentle course for gentlemen."

Murragh O'Brien, who became a member before the war, when annual subscriptions were five pounds a year, and nothing if you were a bond-holder, is as old as the Club itself. A scion of the Anglo-Irish aristocracy, he lives in a house on the edge of Windsor Great Park, which was once the home of the poet Percy Bysshe Shelley. He no longer plays golf, but every Saturday morning he drives the short distance to the Club and walks the 1st hole.

It is a perfect summer's day in early June. The grass glistens with dew and the rhododendrons are in full bloom. Murragh O'Brien opens the boot of his sky blue Rolls Royce and sits on the tailgate to exchange carpet slippers for walking shoes. As we stroll down the fairway, he chats about times gone by. "You see this ditch here," he says pointing to a small channel that cuts across the fairway not far from the 1st tee. "It used to be further on but Lord Derby's wife, who was a keen golfer, couldn't drive over it so she got her husband to have it moved a bit closer.

"My father was mad about golf and I've played it all my life. Mind you, I wouldn't belong to a club where you couldn't bring your dog. I once had a marvellous labrador who had an uncanny knack of finding golf balls although he would never touch a ball in play. I didn't buy a ball for twenty years!

"Swinley was always a very friendly club. Pretty well all the members knew each other in the old days. Just one tee then, no nonsense. You'd bumble up here and play, and if you wanted to say your handicap was 36 no one would question you. Everyone used to have caddies. One old fellow called Boyer was a character who always wore his cap over his ear. He once saw the Rajmata of Jaipur hit an appalling shot on the 15th. She lost her ball and asked Boyer to find it. He looked at her and said: 'If Mrs. Gandhi saw you play that shot, she'd put you back in prison!'

"The 15th reminds me of another story," he says, stopping and looking around approvingly at the deserted course. "There's a steep incline going up to the green. Lord Hardwicke named it 'New Members' Hill': he reckoned that was where old members dropped dead, making room for new ones to join."

Ted Baillieu, who also fought in the war and later had a distinguished career in the City of London, has been a member of Swinley for almost fifty years and was Club chairman for seven of them. Becoming a member in the old days was an arbitrary and casual business. His father was a member and one day he asked the Secretary if he thought young Ted could join. The Secretary conferred with Sir Edward Peacock, then chairman, and reported back. "He said he had told Sir Edward that we had a new person up for membership. Sir Edward asked who proposed him. When he was told, he said that would be all right. He never asked who the candidate was!"

"When I joined," says Ted Baillieu, "there were no more than 250 members and no bar.

Previous pages:
An autumn view of the 11th hole.
Opposite:
The Swinley silver.

Following pages:
Winter golf on the 1st fairway.

When you wanted a drink you pressed a button and the steward would bring you one. The changing room was appalling. There is a story, probably apocryphal but never mind, about some American visitors coming in after their game very hot and very wet. Where could they take a shower? 'No, we don't have showers here,' they were told. 'Their lordships take their baths at home.'"

Both the course and the clubhouse have changed considerably since Murragh O'Brien and Ted Baillieu first joined. The greatest transformation has occurred in the last decade, particularly in the last three years, and coincides in no accidental way with the chairmanship of Ted Baillieu and the arrival of a new Secretary, Ian Pearce. For the older members, those changes are viewed as verging on revolutionary; for the younger just about right and absolutely necessary.

First, the golf course. While Swinley undoubtedly remains a club for gentlemen, its course is no longer "gentle". Originally designed by the great golf architect, H. S. Colt, the Swinley course could not have a more "inland" appearance, since it is carved out of a forest. The magical component is its heathland soil, known as Bagshot sand, a free-draining porous mixture of black soil, grey sand, clay and flint. This means that Swinley does not flood or become waterlogged and its contours are natural and harmonious: it has all the advantages of a links course without the hazards of searing winds and rapacious seas. The many fine golf courses in the area, including Sunningdale, Wentworth and the Berkshire, also owe their existence to this happy geological accident.

In recent years, the course has been toughened up with changes to the bunkers, new tees that extend its length, and a tightening of par on a number of holes. But Swinley was never designed to be a course for championships. The Club rules reinforce this philosophy. A sign in the clubhouse, for the benefit of visiting societies, announces that the Club operates preferred lies throughout the year. "The game of golf here has been made rather simple," says Lawson Bingham, the course manager. "There are no red or yellow posts identifying ditches and other hazards. If you land in one of these places, you have a choice. You either play it or lift and drop under penalty. The fairways are the same." Swinley has always been known for its greens, which are superb. But it never cuts the fairways short, as is done on championship courses. Members like it teed-up a bit.

Ian Pearce, the Club's Secretary, is a former regular army officer who had a distinguished career in army and county golf. He introduced the par scorecard in 1990, eighty-one years after the Club was founded. He describes modern Swinley as "a stern test of golfing ability. You will require every club in the bag to play it successfully. My favourite holes are 9 and 12, two very tough par 4's. I never get tired of playing this course."

Lawson Bingham, a Scot who spent twenty-one years at Prestwick and five at Sunningdale, has been responsible for bringing the course up to a high standard after it went through a bad patch. As a veteran of links and heathland courses, he observes that the most important asset for a greenkeeper is a large dose of common sense. "To be a good greenkeeper, you've got to be very aware of the weather. You've got to work with it and play with it. Machinery and irrigation make life easier, but diplomas are no substitute for experience."

Bob Parker, the Club professional and caddiemaster, has been at Swinley for almost twenty years and succeeded a man who had held the job for more than half a century. He

Opposite top: *Heather-crested bunker.* Opposite: *Forest detail.*

Following pages: *A peaceful foursome.*

Portrait of the 17th Earl of Derby, Swinley's founder, in the Club Room.

can rustle up forty to fifty caddies for society days, if necessary, and does reasonably well in his shop from visiting golfers. But there is far less activity with members, both in sales and in teaching. One old member, he recalls, tried out a pair of socks on the golf course for two days running before deciding to buy two pairs. He didn't pay cash but asked to be billed. Six weeks later, a cheque for £4 arrived. Fourteen years later, the same member came into the shop and said: "I say, Parker, I must get some more socks from you because I think those pairs have worn out."

As for teaching, the demand is slim. "It's hard when you consider the average age of our membership," says Bob Parker. "I remember Sir Archibald Forbes coming in one day. He was 84 and said he'd like a couple of lessons because he wanted to put some length on his drive!"

The changes to Swinley's clubhouse are more dramatic than to the course. "Bits of wood were hanging out of the ceiling," one member says, "it looked like the sunken wreck of Henry VIII's 'Mary Rose.' Absolutely terrifying." Essential structural work had to be done.

Light lunch after a round.

    New red bricks, of the appropriate warm, Edwardian tone, were imported from France. And while new changing rooms, for members and visitors, raised no hackles, a brand new bar was more controversial. One gentleman who was up for membership withdrew in a huff. "I refuse to join a club with a bar like the Hilton," he said.

    The bar is undoubtedly modern, but a long way from Hiltonian kitsch. That apart, the clubhouse retains its old-world atmosphere. The dining-room upstairs has not parted company with its heavy oak tables and chairs; the generous staircase is structurally safer but otherwise unchanged; the club room downstairs remains an oasis of calm in a busy world.

    Other changes to Swinley are the direct result of the imperative to refurbish and renovate. Money had to be raised. "The options for the membership," says Ian Pearce, "were to increase subscriptions dramatically, bring in new members, or utilise the golf course more. The members decided on a combination of all three."

    The result was a doubling of entry fees and annual subscriptions, an increase in the membership from 225 to 325, and more visitors paying higher fees. "Increasing the mem-

Following pages: Rhododendrons in full bloom on the 12th green.

Opposite top: *The 19th Earl of Derby on his first visit to the Club.*
Opposite bottom: *Neil Harman, a younger Swinley member, in the City.*
Above: *Sir John Milne, chairman.*

bership by that amount, in just two years, was revolutionary," admits Pearce. "But most 18-hole golf clubs have a membership of roughly 700, so our figure is still low." These numbers, however, do not give a true picture of actual play at Swinley and many other clubs in this book, because members usually belong to more than one club and divide their play among them.

The Club is now on an even financial keel but not yet sailing free. Rent paid to the Crown for the part of the course it owns will be going up in the near future, and renovations still have to be done to Lawson Bingham's house. (Housing is provided to all members of the Club's staff, on or off the premises.) If all goes well, the strategy is to cut down on the number of visitors' days — currently Monday to Friday — because more elderly members want to play during the week. The intensity of society and corporate play falls on Tuesdays and Thursdays. On Mondays, Wednesdays and Fridays, visitors have to be off the 1st tee by 9.30 am, so that members turning up later can play. Nearly every golf club has to perform this balancing act between society and member play.

Following pages: *Tranquillity.*

One of the results of the dramatic increase in membership has been to bring in younger members, though at Swinley the term "younger" must be used advisedly. The average of Swinley's membership used to be close to seventy. After the new influx, that has come down to fifty-four. Here it is said half-jokingly that a junior member is someone who is close to retirement.

But there are young members at Swinley. One is Neil Harman, who is in his early thirties and works as an insurance broker in the City of London. Both his father and grandfather (a bond holder) were Swinley members. He is also a member of the Royal St. George's, where he plays his competitive golf. "Swinley's completely different," he says. "They have only just started an annual Club competition. There was talk of putting up a championship board for the winners, but it was shot down. 'Too much like a dog club,' one of the committee members complained. My brother is also a member. He's not a keen golfer, and so it's perfect for him. It's a quiet place, not hard to get to, not competitive, a fine place to take his dog for a walk." As for change, says Harman, the younger members of Swinley are broadly in harmony with the older ones. "Some change has to come, but it should not be dramatic. Our view is that if it ain't broke, don't fix it." The new chairman, Sir John Milne, echoes this sentiment: "If I started introducing new things like a Sunday barbecue, I'd be out of a job."

To get on Swinley's waiting list for membership, all you need is two sponsors who are Club members. And golfing prowess? "Golfing ability doesn't come into it," says Ian Pearce. "In fact, if you were a scratch golfer, the view would be, 'oh God, he's going to play a lot!' It's your social attributes that matter." There are no juniors or cadets, so the earliest you can go on the waiting list is eighteen. Once there, the applicant must await the passage of an elderly member to the great fairway in the sky. "You can reckon about ten years on the fast track and fifteen on the slow."

Another shift is the way the Club is run. Swinley used to be ruled by what was proudly known as "a self-perpetuating oligarchy". The Club is currently run by a six-man committee headed by a chairman. It has never had a captain, much less a president. Like most of the traditional clubs, the day-to-day adminstration is handled by the Secretary for the past decade, here Ian Pearce. The oligarchic spirit of the place continues, however, through the chairman who, in consultation with the committee, chooses his own successor. It is also reflected in the residual powers of the bond holders. There are still fifty-three bonds outstanding, and no Club rule can be changed unless two-thirds of the holders assent.

Swinley gentlemen still play golf at their leisure, leisurely. The favoured game is foursomes. The older members tend to play during the week and the younger at weekends. Were it not for the societies and corporate visitors, Swinley would be quite under-used. The not uncommon sight of a totally deserted course on a Saturday or Sunday may baffle the outsider, but it produces a warm glow in the hearts of Swinley members.

Competitive golf is confined to an annual match between the Club and the Fernhill Artisans Golf Club, Swinley's artisan affiliate, and a few societies like the Match Club. The match against the Artisans is played for the Peacock Cup, named after Sir Edward Peacock, a famously imperious chairman of the Club. It is the Club's only real piece of silverware and, not surprisingly, kept well out of sight in the office safe. There are now also two internal competitions: a summer singles match play knockout and a winter foursomes knockout, both played off scratch. Younger members at the committee meeting who pointed out that, apart from the pleasure of competition, this revolutionary idea would be a good way to meet other members, were told by one old guard stalwart: "I didn't join this Club to meet other members!"

A glance down Swinley's list of members, framed in teak and gold and hanging on a wall in the changing room, reveals its blue-blooded lineage. Below the Duke of Edinburgh and his son, the Duke of York, you will find the Duke of Beaufort, the Marquis of Linlithgow, Viscount Dilhorne, Viscount Garmoyle, Viscount Head, the Earls of Clarendon, Woolton and Perth, Lord Hambro, a clutch of knights and honourables and, of course, the nineteenth Earl of Derby, who succeeded to the title in 1994 and maintains the family connection that his great-uncle started. (John Boardman, a distinguished member of the Club — as well as of Sunningdale and the R&A — was once asked by a member how on earth he had managed to join Swinley without either a title or a hyphen in his name.) The small ladies' section, mainly non-playing wives of members, includes Countess Douglas, Lady Agnew, Lady Milne, Lady Rosemary Muir and the redoubtable lady who had trouble at the 15th, the Rajmata of Jaipur.

Members tend to come from the same social background: Eton and Harrow, the Guards and the Greenjackets, Oxford and Cambridge; and belong to the same London clubs: White's, Boodle's and Brooks. They are merchant bankers, stockbrokers, company chairmen and directors, lawyers and landed gentry. Where there is money, it is old money. Here, as in all the traditional clubs, wealth is never talked about nor flaunted, and it is easier for a golf buggy to pass through the eyelet of a golf shoe than to buy your way into Swinley Forest.

With the old money goes a patrician style. "The majority are very nice," says Geoffrey Holmberg, who is a part-time steward in the Club and even older than many of the members. "They treat you as an equal," he says. Bob Parker has some experience with the minority. "There's one chap here," he observes, "who, if he came into my shop, looked over the counter and found that I had dropped dead on the floor, would say: 'I say, Parker's dead. Who's looking after the caddies?'"

One story sums up the nature of Swinley's membership. A visiting society player is talking with a Swinley member in the changing-room. "Yes," he says, "we have a nice cross-section of people in my club."

"Oh do you," replies the Swinley member. "We haven't got that problem here."

There are no cocktail parties or evening events at Swinley, and, although Club rules allow card-playing, no one can remember ever seeing that done. The social high point of the week at Swinley is lunch on Saturday and Sunday, when excellent, quintessentially English food is served. "Nursery cooking at its best," said one veteran of the course and the table, "and exactly what the members want." Swinley is also proud of a rather horrible soft drink, called the Swinley Special, the sort of concoction that children in the nursery mixed up when Nanny's back was turned. It seems to refresh after a hot day out on the course, and members profess to like it.

Swinley is a lovely place to play friendly golf. Here members can just turn up, at any time, and know that they can play. For as long as that continues to happen, Swinley men will know that the Club has got things right.

Prestwick caddies.

Clean, Sober and Wise: The Caddie

[Definition: "Caddie" or "Cadie" from the French "cadet", meaning a porter or an odd-job man.]

The bad news is that caddies are a dying breed; the good news is that those who are left either don't know it or, if they do, refuse to let it worry them. Eight out of the twelve traditional golf clubs surveyed in this book have caddies as much, if not more, for the benefit of their visitors than of their members. At most clubs these days, members carry their own bags or use hand or battery-assisted trolleys, and the professionals usually have their own caddies. British golfers, American visitors will note, do not believe in motorised buggies — although the larger clubs will keep a few, discreetly out of sight, strictly for the use of the aged and infirm.

Snowball — he admits to no other name — was virtually born a caddie, first seeing the light of day "just to the right of the 7th fairway." His grandfather was the car park attendant at Sunningdale and his father, Blondie, was a caddie all his life. Snowball, who has been caddying at the Club since the early 1960s, has an almost piratical appearance — hair down to his shoulders, comprehensively bearded, be-ringed fingers — and a knowing air. "I learnt to work with me eyes but the young new fellers are lookin' at the numbers," he says rubbing his forefinger and thumb together suggestively. "That's one of the reasons golfers bring their own caddies with 'em these days."

Snowball, in the best traditions of his profession, is not only knowledgeable about the golf courses he works on, but on Club lore. "King Edward VIII used to live near here after his abdication," he says lighting up a cigarette. "The butler nicked the jools and buried them over there to the right of the 17th green."

Reg Barton, now retired and breaching eighty, began caddying at the Royal Liverpool Golf Club in 1930, the year Bobby Jones won the Grand Slam. "In the 1930s," he says, "there would be fifty men and boys lining up outside the clubhouse." He later caddied for Ben Crenshaw ("grand chap, he was, got dressed up in a Scottish kilt in the evenings") and worked regularly at the Club until his retirement. The most dramatic moment of his career was not during a championship

Top: *St. George's caddies.* Above: *R&A caddies.*

or international match but when the Captain of the Club, for whom he was caddying at the time, dropped dead at the 5th tee. His last caddying job was for Prince Andrew, the Duke of York. On hearing that we might be meeting the Prince at Swinley Forest, Reg Barton's ears pricked up. "Oh, if you do see him, ask him for my pencil. He never gave it back."

Brian McGowne, a flaxen-haired, red-faced caddie who looks as if he might have had Viking ancestors, has caddied all over Scotland but is now settled at Prestwick Golf Club in Ayrshire. He combines a deep knowledge of Prestwick's intimidating links with a fund of stories which he uses to relax the nervous first-time customers. "We play golf twelve months a year at Prestwick," he says, "and when the Americans ask me aboot rain, I tell 'em it only rained twice this year, once for six months and the other time for four months."

It is unlikely that the tradition of caddies, so much part of the history of golf, will die out completely. Demand remains fairly constant at clubs like Sunningdale, Sandwich and Prestwick, and bodies can usually be found, although their golfing expertise and knowledge of the course may be severely limited. "How's your eyesight?" seems to be a more common question from a golfer to an unknown caddie these days than, say, "What's the best approach to the 3rd green?" And whatever happens in the amateur game will not change the professionals' reliance upon their right-hand men (or women) who trundle along beside them, through thick and thin, and provide all the traditional nourishment — technical, psychological and, when required, philosophical — which the best caddies have always brought to the game.

And should the caddie finally share the fate of the dodo, it is re-assuring to know that people who write about golf are unlikely to let the fact of physical extinction stand in their way. Caddie stories, fact and fiction and already legion, will surely multiply no matter what. There is no space for a representative sample here, but there is room for one joke. This concerns a bad and irascible golfer who, seeking a scapegoat for his own incompetence, turns to his patient caddie when it is all over. "You must be the worst caddie in the world!" he bursts out. "That," says the caddie calmly, "would be too much of a coincidence."

197.

A Nine-Hole Wonder

Royal Worlington and Newmarket Golf Club

"It is a little triangle of dry, sandy, 'seaside' land in the flat heart of rural Suffolk, complete with gorse and fir trees, just big enough for nine holes," wrote Henry Longhurst, in his autobiography, *My Life and Soft Times*. "Who laid them out I do not know . . . but either he was a man of genius or he brought off a gigantic fluke, for Mildenhall, in my experience, is comparable only with the Old Course at St. Andrews." It might seem odd that a 9-hole golf course should be in the same league — or indeed the same book — as conventional 18-hole courses. But the Club once commonly known as Mildenhall and now usually referred to by its short name Worlington, is in a class of its own. Bernard Darwin called it "the sacred nine" — a phrase borrowed for the title of the Club's centenary history — and other golf sages down the years, from Herbert Warren Wind to Pat Ward-Thomas to Sir Michael Bonallack have wholeheartedly agreed.

The clubhouse and course are tucked away between wheat fields and the quiet village of Worlington, about six miles from Newmarket and twenty miles from Cambridge. Imagine that you played here fifty years ago, perhaps as a Cambridge undergraduate. Your first impressions on returning would be to question your memory; yet everything is as you saw it then. The famous bunkerless 5th hole has not changed in any significant way nor, on closer inspection, have any of the other 8 holes. The picturesque farmhouse that has served as a clubhouse for over a century continues to reflect its original use as faithfully as ever.

You walk in, cross the familiar worn flagstones exactly as you might have done half a century earlier, stand in front of a serving hatch, which still measures two feet by two and a half feet, and order a "pink jug", the special Club drink. Served from an ornate Victorian water jug, the ingredients of this cooling but potent concoction have not changed either: a bottle of champagne, equal tots of Benedictine, brandy and Pimm's No. 1, lemon and ice. Reassuringly, the pink jug remains the Club emblem, uncluttered against a navy blue background on members' ties and on the Club flag.

The steward's face will not be familiar, but the liquid refreshment, the wholesome and tasty home-made food and everything else in the clubhouse, down to the roller-towels, wooden toilet seats and pock-marked benches in the changing room, will match the image lodged in your brain, detail by faithful detail. Surely, something must have altered in fifty years? Well, if you want to be pedantic, yes, there is a new clock — celebrating the Club's centenary in 1993 — on the front of the clubhouse; and, yes, a light cord has been replaced in the changing-room (the new one appropriately weighted with a golf ball); and, yes, one of those flagstones directly in front of the hatch has been turned over due to wear. But that's it.

This 9-hole wonder was founded in May 1893 by two members of the local landed gentry: a Captain (later Brigadier General) E. W. D. Baird, and Harry McCalmont who, after Eton, had served in the Scots Guards. The land, which included a small farmhouse ideal for conversion to a clubhouse, belonged to William Gardner, who became one of twenty founder members.

The Club acquired its royal patronage in 1895, a mere two years after its foundation. But in 1901 William Gardner decided to sell much of his property, including the course and the clubhouse. The Club thus experienced the ignominy of finding itself on the auction block in Newmarket, billed as "Lot 5 . . . The Royal Worlington and Newmarket Golf Links, reputed to be the most perfect Nine-hole Golf course in the Country." Luckily, the lot failed to sell and two years later the Club bought the property for £2,677, placing its destiny firmly in the hands of the membership.

The mystery surrounding the identity of the creator of the golf course was only finally resolved a hundred years after the event when John Gillum, Worlington's president, started researching and writing the Club's centenary history in the early 1990s. It was not, as many thought, Willie Park, the designer of the Old Course at Sunningdale. Nor was it Tom Hood, Worlington's first professional, steward and greenkeeper. Rather it was an English professional golfer called Tom Dunn, a prolific designer of golf courses known for exclaiming when he cast his eye over a new prospect: "God meant this land to be a golf course."

The phrase cannot have been justified on every occasion, but there is no doubt that Tom Dunn hit the nail on the head at Worlington. Like the Bagshot sand southwest of London, a thin band of sand runs through Suffolk ("a golf stream," poet and golfer Patric Dickinson called it), and this provided Dunn with the raw material to craft and build a course fifty miles from the North Sea, which, like links courses, is playable all year round. The course, apart from acquiring an extra 441 yards in length, has changed little over time. The principal changes were made over seventy years ago under the direction of the renowned H. S. Colt. The holes most affected were the 4th, 8th and 9th. The last hole, where the bottom of the flag was invisible from the tee, had led to the practice, John Gillum reports in the Club history, of the caddies, who had gone forward, turning "a good shot into an even better one, by kicking their masters' ball into the hole." The hole was lengthened and a new, fully visible green built across the road next to the clubhouse.

Some sixty years after Colt's modifications, Herbert Warren Wind paid tribute to Worlington with a lengthy profile in *The New Yorker* in 1981. He included a hole-by-hole description and, since nothing of substance has changed, a few snapshots from that panorama might be illuminating "The 1st, a par 5, is 484 yards long, and . . . is rather routine," he began. "The 2nd, a 225 yard par 3 . . . is a beauty [because of] the bowler

Previous pages:
Late summer evening at Worlington.
Opposite:
The "pink jug".

Following pages:
A foursome at the 1st tee.

Putting on the famous 5th green. *Summer flowers.*

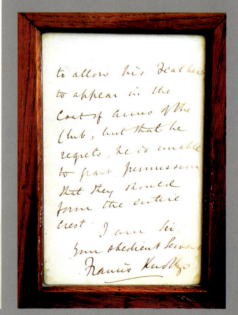

These pages: *Club memorabilia.*

Following pages:
A sudden shower on the 4th/6th fairway.

The Queen at work. July 17th 1893.

Presented to
The Royal Worlington & Newmarket Golf Club
Centenary 1893-1993
by
The Royal Household Golf Club

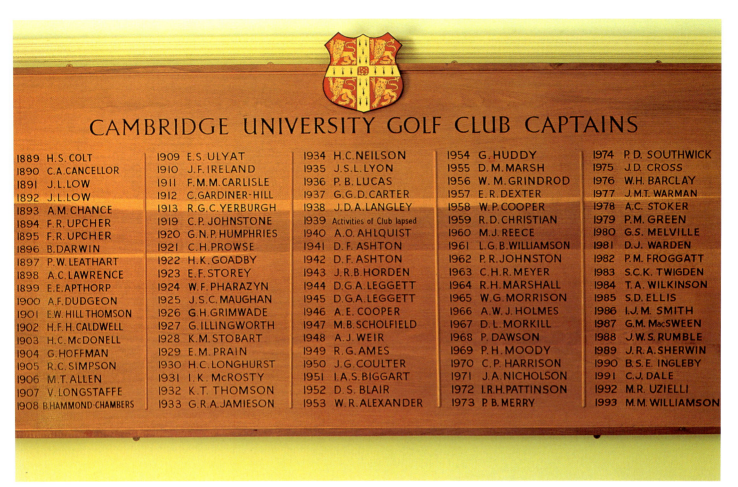

Cambridge University Club captains board at Worlington.

hat, or upturned saucer green. . . . The 3rd is one of the finest of the course. . . . The 4th is like no other par 5 I know . . . with a tiny green. . . . The 5th, 170 yards, par 3, is rated by many of the game's cognoscenti as one of the best par 3s in golf. It is surely one of the most difficult. There isn't a bunker on it, and if there were it would be superfluous . . . the green is exceedingly lean and falls away abruptly on both sides.

"The 6th, the first of two rigorous long par 4s is 455 yards long… the green is tilted toward the golfer, and the key bunker is precisely where it should be — twenty-five feet from the left front edge of the green. It does a lot of business. . . . The 7th, 165 yards long, is the poorest of Worlington's three par 3s, but on most courses it would be a standout. . . . The 8th, the second of the rousing long par 4s — 465 yards — owes its character to the inspired retention of an archaic hazard, a crossbunker that thrusts itself up above the level of the fairway and runs clear across it eighty-five yards from the front of the green. . . . The 9th . . . is a dogleg par 4, . . . with a stream that purls along the right side of the fairway. . . . The green is small and . . . its surface is a froth of dips and bumps — there is hardly a straight putt on it."

The course record is held by Jo Floyd, whose scorecard, for the lowest nine holes at Worlington, is framed on the clubhouse wall. On 3 September 1949, playing off a handicap of 2, he went round in an astonishing 28. He doesn't recall much about the actual golf except that after he got an albatross two at the 1st hole, he thought, "this could be my day." For the other 8 holes he notched up an eagle, four birdies and three pars.

Dr. Omar Malik and Paul Guest, Cambridge captains, at the University.

Like Rye, a genuine seaside links course, Worlington is at its best in winter, when most other inland courses are soggy swamps or mired in mud. The greens, extraordinarily fast, are the jewel in the crown and lovingly cared for by Bob Gee, the head greenkeeper who was born in nearby Mildenhall and has worked at the Club for nearly forty years. "The greens are their best in winter," he says, "and if there's a little frost on them, we still let people play. Greenkeeping is the science of the climate not the calendar, and cannot be done by a rule book."

"The greens are sheer poetry," wrote the poet Patric Dickinson. "They are like swimming in a mountain lake, as compared with the sea. The approach must be clean, the putt perfectly timed and struck: then the reward — to stand and watch, *with certainty*, the long putt going home to the bottom — a marvellous clear-water feeling. I know of no other greens that are so utterly scrupulous. Putting upon them is a sheer aesthetic delight — in one's own skill pitted against the best of the greenkeeper's. If Plato had played golf, here was the place for him Ideally to Putt."

The Cambridge University connection with Worlington is almost as old as the Club itself (it officially dates from 1901). University golfers can practise on a weekly basis at Worlington and play all their home matches at the Club. The number of Cambridge golfers is limited to twenty-four but this allows all members of the two teams — the Blues and the Stymies, plus a few reserves — to use the course. After they leave Cambridge, all golfing Blues have a reasonable expectation of being elected to full membership at a

Above and opposite: *Changing-room details*.

concessionary subscription, currently about half the normal rate, and no entrance fee.

Paul Guest, the Cambridge Captain (1997–98) and his immediate predecessor, Omar Malik (1996–97), talk about Worlington in the cosy clubroom of the Hawks Club, the prestigious preserve of Cambridge's top sportsmen, over an exceptionally good pot of coffee. Worlington provides superb preparation for the varsity match, which is invariably played on links courses, points out Guest. "Oxford don't have that advantage," he says, "nor do they have the contact with their immediate predecessors that we get through the former golf Blues at Worlington. We learn a lot from them."

Malik believes that Worlington's 9 holes provide a special advantage in preparing the Cambridge team for competitive golf, because playing the same 9 holes twice at Worlington requires a similar mental discipline to playing 18 holes twice in the Varsity Match. "And the greens are special, very fast, very contoured, and very difficult to read. At Worlington you are playing the demons."

Traditionally, a senior member of Worlington is designated to act as an informal liaison officer between Club and university. He is always a former Blue and a member of the Oxford and Cambridge Golfing Society. The relationship between Cambridge golfers and the Club membership has been remarkably smooth over the years but problems arose in the early 1990s. "It was forgotten that playing at Royal Worlington was a privilege given to us and not a right," says Malik. "Since then it's become a practise for the Captain to brief a new undergraduate about the Club. You've got to turn up there looking

respectable. You can't look as if you have just rolled out of bed having had a few pints the night before."

"Worlington is a funny place," adds Guest. "It's very traditional but it's also very informal."

In the old days, Cambridge golfers used to reach the Club by the railway, the Mildenhall branch that gave the Club its popular name in university golfing circles, and which closed in 1962. The line passed close to the 5th tee and until 1922 when a train stop was created near the clubhouse, undergraduates used to toss their clubs out of the window as the train chugged by to save carrying them back to the course.

The Club's pride in its Cambridge golfers is demonstrated by the support that members give to the team when it plays here at its home base and the honour boards in the dining-room listing the Captains of the Cambridge University Golf Club, dating back to H. S. Colt in 1889. For its part, Cambridge has produced some remarkable golfers and golf writers who went on to become either enthusiastic members of Worlington or lifelong admirers of the Club. The exalted gallery includes Bernard Darwin, Eustace Storey, Leonard Crawley, Eric Martin Smith, Henry Longhurst, Patric Dickinson, Laddie Lucas, John Langley, Donald Steel, Gordon Huddy, Brian Chapman and David Marsh.

Laddie Lucas, a remarkably talented left-handed Walker Cup player, World War II fighter pilot ace, politician, businessman and writer, recalled his Cambridge days at Worlington with passion and poignancy in his book on golf, *The Sport of Princes*. "On

Top: *The Hatch: Mr. Wright at your service.*
Above left: *Mr. and Mrs. Wright before retirement.*
Above right: *Bob Gee, greenkeeper.*
Opposite top: *Club quorum.*
Opposite center left: *Daniel Griggs.*
Opposite center right: *Mrs. Liz Boatman with her daughter Alex.*
Opposite bottom left: *J. R. (John) Gillum, Club president and historian.*
Opposite bottom right: *Dr. B. J. (John) Batt (far right), with friends.*

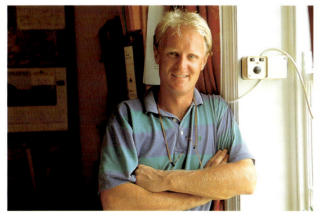

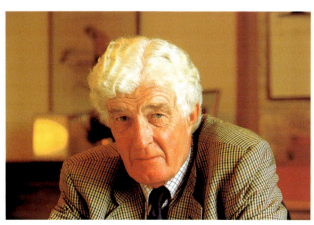

and on we played, enveloped in nostalgia. . . . Every hole had some association, some incident, some remark, some chance word of wisdom, some shot to recapture and savour again. . . ."

Worlington, like its East Anglian cousin, Brancaster, has a small but highly active ladies' section and a tradition of being benign to women golfers in general. Liz Boatman first played at Worlington when she was seventeen years old. "It's one of those courses when you first play it, you think, well, this is a bit of a doddle," she says. "But the more you play it, the more difficult it becomes." She should know, having been a county champion, an English international and twice captain of the British and Irish Curtis Cup team.

"Worlington is full of extremely nice people with a very friendly atmosphere," continues Boatman, who still plays off a handicap of 3. "If you're a stranger walking into Worlington, you won't be left sitting on your own for very long. Weekends can be like a big private cocktail party — immense fun. And we've got a really super ladies' section, one of the nicest in the country, a total of about sixty of whom thirty or so play."

Her daughter, Alex Boatman, a classics scholar at Cambridge as well as an accomplished sportswoman, says there is no "chauvinist nonsense" at Royal Worlington, unlike many other traditional golf clubs she has visited as player or guest. "There are no restrictions at all as to where women can go — except the men's changing-room, which is fine! The vote will come in time, I am sure, because the Club is full of forward-looking people and they're such good people."

Worlington's membership is what you might expect, a blend of local retired people, some farmers, a smattering of the racing community from nearby Newmarket, the former Cambridge Blues and some London professional people. There is a junior section composed of sons and daughters of members who, together with the current Cambridge University players, inject an element of youth into the Club. There is no waiting list but few vacancies because of a policy of firmly restricting membership to preserve the course and to enable members to come along at virtually any time and be sure of a game. Visitors are welcomed, but society activity is limited to about twenty days a year; there are no corporate or hospitality days.

Ian Pattinson, who has been both a Captain of Cambridge and Worlington and is an active member of the R&A, believes Worlington's secret lies in its ability to maintain a compact, friendly and mutually-respectful membership. "People know each other here," he says, "in fact, it's very unusual to come into the clubhouse and *not* know everyone there." Play is foursomes and singles — three- and four-ball is banned — and uncompetitive; only a handful of members turn up for the monthly medal. "Cambridge University provides the cutting edge here as far as the golf goes," says Pattinson.

Worlington has a unique and slightly bizarre Club competition played every December called "Whisky and Walnuts." As members arrive at the Club they are randomly formed into five-person teams without regard to gender. The Captains of each team assign each member one golf club for the alternate shots contest — which is played twice over three unorthodox holes: 1st tee to 2nd green; 3rd tee to 4th green; 5th tee to 9th green. Thirty to forty teams typically vie for the winner's bottle of whisky and the runner-up's bag of walnuts.

On a warm summer's day the poppy-strewn wheat and barley fields of Suffolk seem to have fallen asleep. Contented cattle, up to their ears in wild flowers, lie under hedgerows chewing the cud. Even the fighter jets of the Mildenhall air-base have decided to take a siesta. But down at Worlington it is a lively scene. The Old Lags (a golfing society of London arbitration judges and lawyers), who are pitting their golfing wits against the Jailbirds (another society whose essential qualification is to have spent at least twenty-four hours in jail), are preparing to go out for the afternoon round. Mr. Wright, the Club steward, is busy behind his hatch serving "pink jugs", pints of bitter and glasses of kummel to the golfers, who have just demolished an excellent lunch prepared by Mrs. Wright.

A group of members is having drinks after playing a round in the Winter Foursomes, a Club competition conducted at so leisurely a pace that one annual competition is often still being finished after the next is well under way.

A younger member is explaining that he spends more time playing golf with older members than his peers. "Oh, that's because most of them are out working for a living," says his older partner with a laugh.

"No, it's just that I prefer playing with the older crowd," says the younger man. "It's like a lot of women who prefer men's company to women's. Well, I like the company of older people rather than those my own age."

"What, you like old women!" Laughter erupts and more drinks are ordered.

Someone asks if are there any "four letter men" at Worlington.

"I don't think so," says the older member.

"I've never experienced any prejudice against me," says an American member.

"Damn Yanks!" says the older member.

"If someone were a bore here," says another member, "he'd be told pretty quickly to stop being one or push off."

The older member and his American partner are competing in the Winter Foursomes but seem in no hurry. "It's cut-throat stuff," says the older member.

"This is the first round," says the younger member. "It should have been completed by 31 December last year and it's now mid-July."

Just then their opponents come up and one of them steps forward. "Gentlemen, we've come to offer you a quadruple kummel and to say that we'll be teeing off in two minutes."

There is no question that Worlington sits comfortably within its own skin, and readily shares its human quality and inner warmth with outsiders. "Worlington is a magic place that somehow has maintained the tradition of people enjoying themselves," said Jo Floyd. "It is small and it is beautiful."

More than a century old, this golfing curiosity looks ahead to another hundred years with confidence. Should there be any doubts in a visitor's mind, a glance at the Cambridge University Golf Club Captains boards in the dining room will settle the matter. The old board is full, but two new ones have been put up which, between them, can accommodate Cambridge Captains for the entire twenty-first century and still leave room for a few more.

A Family Affair

Royal West Norfolk Golf Club

The first hint of something unusual came in the timbered bar of the Lifeboat Inn at Thornham. Adrian Brown, journalist and golfer, looked up from his pint when he heard we were planning to visit his club, the Royal West Norfolk. "Have you checked the tide?" he asked earnestly.

The turn off the main coastal road towards the Club is marked by St. Mary the Virgin, Brancaster's fourteenth-century parish church. The road descends gently and immerses itself in tall reeds and marsh grasses as it seeks out the dunes and the sea beyond. A suspicious dampness on a bone-dry day tells the story of the tide; it is ebbing fast after sealing off the road to the course and clubhouse for an hour or more. Ahead lie the dunes and the links with the flags snapping in the wind. And then, dead in front, the clubhouse, a brave, bizarre building that only the Victorians could have concocted, exposed on all sides to the elements and sitting defiantly on a pile of rocks with the sea at its feet.

"It is a fine bracing spot with a grand sandy beach for children," wrote a founding father of the Club in 1893. "There is nothing finer in its way than the view from the 9th hole under a blue sky, and that alone is worth a visit."

Today a golfer on the elevated 9th tee would find that lovely view little changed, like so much here. One sees an untrammelled, harmonious landscape, a seamless tapestry of sea, sky and land unexpectedly enhanced by man's own artefacts on the links and the hinterland. The broad sea-scrubbed beach stretches for miles in both directions. Its vastness effortlessly absorbs the holiday-makers, wind-surfers and dog-walkers, but most of the time it is as it ever was: a pristine seascape where the timeless rhythm of the tides below and the birds above are the only activity.

Off the coast looms Scolt Head, a sandy spit growing daily as the tides shift sand from one part of the coast to another. Turn inland and the channel that connects the picturesque harbour of Brancaster Staithe with the open sea comes into view. This is likely to be flecked with sailing boats while others bob and sway in the harbour against a backdrop of ancient red-roofed houses, barns and farm buildings. Beyond, the land rises gently demonstrating that not all Norfolk is boringly flat. An orderly perspective unfolds:

wheat and barley fields, fresh and green in the spring sunshine, the occasional golden splash of rape-seed, and the darker green of woods and copses where pheasant and partridge abound.

It was this peaceful corner of England that Holcombe Ingelby and his brother Herbert, accompanied by a small group of golfing friends, chanced upon in the winter of 1891. The proprietor and lord of the manor, W. H. Simms-Reeve, was quickly transformed into an enthusiastic supporter of the idea of a golf links, even though he had never seen a golf ball. Negotiations were rapidly and satisfactorily concluded with Brancaster Village over its ancient common grazing rights; a course was laid out by "the great Horace" Hutchinson; the royal patronage of the Prince of Wales (the future Edward VIII) was secured; an iron hut was bought for £45 to serve as a temporary clubhouse; and officers were appointed. W. H. Simms-Reeve was the president and Horace Hutchinson, the new Club's first Captain. The conception, birth and royal baptism of the Royal West Norfolk Golf Club was accomplished within two months.

Brancaster had everything except members. The Club's committee had promised the local villagers to elect "none but gentlemen in every sense of the word, that is men of integrity and honour." Word went out among the Norfolk squirearchy and London's clubland, and by the end of the 1892, 270 gentlemen golfers had joined. The first hundred were admitted free of charge; those who followed paid an annual subscription of one guinea.

Who were these early members? Rather similar, in fact, to the current membership, which is made up of professional men from London (lawyers, bankers, doctors), landed gentry from Norfolk and other parts of East Anglia, some military men (with the Royal Air Force in the ascendant) and local farmers. The Club also has an aristocratic patina with a mixture of peers and knights and a significant royal connection. Former Captains include a Prince of Wales and three dukes. The Duke of Kent, Captain in 1981, and the Duke of York, are still members.

Brancaster has had a reputation for being exclusive and snobbish. Nigel Carrington-Smith, a former army infantry officer who has been Secretary for more than a decade, says it's not so. "We do have a number of titled people and a certain amount of private wealth, old money rather than new. But there are no pretensions here. Generation follows generation, sons follow their fathers. It's not a matter of class or being elitist. It's a self-perpetuating thing. Our Captain calls it the right infrastructure. Norfolk is a well-knit county and we are like a family. Wives and children have always been welcome here."

If ever an individual can personify a golf club, Tom Harvey must be a leading candidate. When he glances at Brancaster's Captains' Board in the Smoke Room, he can count seventeen members of his family over the years, including his grandfather, his father, his brother, his son David and himself. Tom's grandfather was one of the earliest members of Brancaster and his parents were keen golfers too, so keen that they spent their honeymoon in the Dormy House.

Tom Harvey's career and life-style not only epitomise Brancaster, but reflect the timeless England from which the Club draws the bulk of it membership. A modest, erudite and witty man, he served with distinction in the Scots Guards during the Second World War, was later private secretary to the Queen, and married into the local aristocracy. His

Previous pages:
Father and sons putting on the 1st green.
Opposite:
The distinctive Rolph trophy.

Following pages:
A distant view of Brancaster's clubhouse, from the east.

own comfortable eighteenth-century home is embraced by glorious gardens and pristine Norfolk meadows and woodland. He has been the Captain of the R&A and, as chairman of the Championship Committee, organised the Open and the Amateur from 1959 through 1961.

Jo Floyd had similar deep family connections to the Club. "I've been a member since 1932, first as a junior and then, from 1938, as a full member," he said. "It's my favourite golf course and my spiritual home. My grandfather was a member, my parents too. I have two daughters who are members and some grandsons and daughters who are hoping to join. You keep going back to Brancaster, it gets hold of you. I love it. To me it's home." Floyd died on 20 February 1998.

The golf links that the members of the Club love and seek to preserve provide a severe test of the golfer's skill, but are too short for championship events. No one, however, seems to mind that. Golf for enjoyment's sake in a natural setting, often in wild and windy conditions, is the name of the game at Brancaster. Horace Hutchinson called it "a course of exceptional severity not so much to the scratch player as the classes behind him." Writing almost seventy years later, Pat Ward-Thomas, a former Brancaster Captain, caught the essence of the place: "For [golf's] blessings to be complete there must be an element of seclusion. Brancaster has this in far greater measure than most. A golfer can pursue the game's challenge there in a setting of severe, simple beauty that has escaped all but natural change since the beginning of time."

While so much at Brancaster is virtually unchanged — the clubhouse, the character of the membership, the style of the Club — the course has undergone considerable "natural change", most of it dictated by the demands of the wind and the sea. Walking the fairways with Ray Kimber, a visitor hears not only the expertise of the Club's golfing pro, but the additional perspectives from his passions as a naturalist and amateur meteorologist.

"The course is still very unspoilt with the greens posing a special challenge," he says. "The best holes are the 3rd, 8th, 9th and 14th." The 9th is particularly formidable. The green, which sits up high, is protected not only by a towering bunker lined with old railway sleepers — a characteristic of the course — but also by a hazard which fills with sea water as the tide comes in.

"When someone calls me up for a lesson," Ray Kimber says, "the first thing I do is take a look at the tide table. The road could be covered with four to five feet of water — we have tides up to twenty-five feet here. Once someone misjudged the tide and later we saw his car floating around the marshes. The winds also can be pretty powerful, up to thirty miles an hour." Ray Kimber stops on the 9th green. "Look at that lovely light," he exclaims, "so much sky. The summer nights are long here and once I came out and played a round at 4.30 am."

Brancaster's relationship with the sea is a complex love affair that gives the links their special allure but at the same time places them in constant jeopardy. In Ray Kimber's thirty-odd years at the Club, the old lifeboat station, some WWII gun emplacements and the 17th tee, in all some forty yards of terrain, have been lost to the sea. The 1st and 13th greens are under serious threat and the clubhouse, once set comfortably back from the beach, is now on an embattled promontory. In 1927 2 holes were lost to the sea and

Opposite: *Ray Kimber, Club professional.*

Following pages:
A golfer's view of serene West Norfolk, from the 3rd green, looking south.
A long putt witnessed, 9th green.

A golfer's lunch.

The Smoke Room.

Following pages: *The 10th green.*

J. A. (Jo) Floyd, former captain.

Brancaster's worst storm this century, in 1942, put paid to the 11th hole which had to be reconstructed further inland. The defences require constant attention and are a continuous burden on the Club's resources.

But there are some compensations. At the far end of the course, the dunes are actually building. Also as the dunes age, the marram grass slowly dies. "This can be seen on the right side of the 14th hole," says Ray Kimber. "The rough has become much thinner through natural causes. A wild slice off the tee, which would have meant a lost ball twenty years ago, now goes relatively unpunished."

The course, especially in summer, is a tapestry of colour, texture and smell. There are marram and lyme grasses, seablite and sea buckthorn bushes, pale green sea holly, bell-shaped sea campion flowers, Japanese roses, mouse ear, yellow rattle, sea pinks, violet sea lavender, yellow perfumed ladies bedstraw and sea purslane, which exudes an aromatic smell when you crush it underfoot looking for an errant ball. And, if you close your eyes for a moment, you will hear the plaintive call of the gulls and the chattering voices of a dozen different species of birds.

Brancaster has had its share of golfing luminaries: three Walker Cup players — Gerald Micklem, P. B. "Laddie" Lucas and Arthur Perowne — and several members who played at county level with distinction. But Brancaster does not aspire to competitive golf. "At a weekend medal competition recently only thirteen people turned up," says the Secretary.

Brancaster's games are foursomes and singles; a notice banning four-ball matches and leaving three-ball games to the Secretary's discretion stands next to the first tee. This pol-

T. C. (Tom) Harvey, former captain of Brancaster and the R&A, and his son, D. V. (David) Harvey, also a former captain of the Club.

icy makes for companionship and speed of play. "Brancaster is light-bag golf and all about relaxing and enjoying the game and one's companions in a setting of spectacular beauty," says one of the members.

The occasional matches are against long-standing rivals: the Brancaster Village Golf Club, which shares the course, the Guards, the Oxford and Cambridge Golfing Society, other Norfolk clubs and exotics such as A League of Gentlemen, The Ferrets, the I. Zingari Cricket Club, the Pedagogues, the Old Stoic Golfing Society and the Stompers. One of the curiosities of the Royal West Norfolk Golf Club, which adds to its somewhat Alice-in-Wonderland image, is the Backwards Competition. This takes place in October every year and par is 72, instead of 71 for the more orthodox route.

"We have few restrictions here, no start times, no Captain's time to play, no reserved parking places," observes a member. "The joy of this place is that the course is often empty and you can turn up 99 percent of the time and tee-off without waiting. But, in order to preserve all that, we have to restrict the number of members."

There are 730 members in all — 410 men, 120 ladies, and 75 juniors (almost entirely sons and daughters of members), with the balance being made up of overseas, honorary and non-playing members. But the active core is only around 200 members, and is centred on the retired community who play every Tuesday, Thursday and Saturday mornings, the farmers and the holiday fraternity who often have second homes in the area. It's a very homogenous Club without cliques. "We try to make it so that anyone who walks in here can talk to anybody else whether he's 78 or 18, or whether he's a

Top: *Memorial gate at the entrance of the course.*
Above left: *The Captains' Board, 1892-1972.*
Above right: *Mrs. Margaret Freeth, ladies' captain, at the 1st tee.*
Opposite: *Mr. and Mrs. Stephen Walton and family in front of the clubhouse.*

Following pages: *Clubhouse at sunset.*

237.

farmer, a doctor or a lawyer," says Nigel Carrington-Smith, the Club Secretary.

Up until 1988 the Club took in new members without a wait. Then came the boom in golf and the course could not handle it. So the Club laid down some rules and guidelines for weekends, kept the traditional matches, and did not take on any new ones. A ceiling was put on the membership and a waiting-list began. Currently, there are some 300 people on it and, with only fifteen new vacancies every year, the purgatorial delay varies between ten and fifteen years. Juniors reaching the age of 21 usually fill half the vacant places — they are automatically offered membership if they want it — and only half a dozen or so "outsiders" get in annually.

Brancaster has only had four professionals in more than a century of existence. The first was Albert Tingey, who combined the job with that of head greenkeeper. After he left in 1898, the legendary Tom Morris at St. Andrews recommended a young man in his clubmaking and repair shop called Tom King. Tom Senior ruled his staff and caddies somewhat autocratically for three decades but he was fearless when it came to his employees' rights. According to the Club history, if a caddie hadn't been paid on time, "he would stride round to one of the windows in the Smoke Room, tap peremptorily and, if necessary, repeatedly, until the offending player came forth and stumped up."

At the age of 13, Tom King's youngest, Tom Junior, left school to become his father's assistant. He was Norfolk's professional champion from 1925 to 1927 when his father died and he took over as Club professional. Apart from being a fine player and teacher, he was a consummate craftsman of golf clubs, one of the last of his kind in Britain. He spent his entire life at the Club and died in 1966, ending a 67-year reign by the King family that had spanned the rule of four monarchs. Ray Kimber stepped into the King dynasty's shoes and has carried on its traditions, adding a love and deep knowledge of the flora and fauna of the Norfolk coast.

Ray Kimber has also played a part in establishing good relations with Brancaster village where he has many contacts and interests. The Club–village relationship has fluctuated over the years. On the village side at issue were the ancient rights to graze horses, cattle and sheep and to pick samphire (a kind of wild asparagus) and marsh lavender, and access to the course for members of the Brancaster Village Golf Club. For the Club, the problem was to accommodate local interests while maintaining its privacy. Relations, which deteriorated after the Second World War, have much improved since Ray Kimber's arrival, and are now thoroughly amicable.

Village club members can play the course in the late afternoons and evenings and spirited matches between the two clubs are a regular and popular feature of Brancaster's golfing calendar. The essential unity of the two communities is nowhere displayed more poignantly than on the Club's memorial gates. Carved in York stone are the names of the members of both clubs who fell in two world wars, intermingled without club or social distinction, side-by-side in a common patriotic death.

Unlike many traditional clubs, ladies' golf has always been a feature of Brancaster's Club life and never a controversial issue. As early as 1895, the Club records reveal the election of two ladies and by 1904 provision was made for up to thirty lady members. In 1973 the Club joined the English Ladies Golf Association and the first Lady Captain, Lady Walker, was appointed. There are now 120 lady members but only eighty with handicaps and a much smaller nucleus of serious golfers. The ladies run their own part of the Club separately from the men, and have no voting rights. Men decide on the admittance of new lady members.

Do the ladies want to change this? "I think not," says Margaret Freeth, the Lady Captain who is a serious and competitive golfer. "If we became part of the whole Club, we would lose our identity." There is no discrimination when it comes to the juniors and future membership. "Girls with family connections in the Club are automatically invited to become full members, just like the boys," says Margaret Freeth. "That is why it is such a family club."

Brancaster has been called a living museum but that impression would be quickly dispelled if you happened to walk into the clubhouse at lunchtime. You might, however, be put off by the building itself. L.E. Jones, an enthusiast of the course and the setting, had this to say in his book *Georgian Afternoons*. "One eyesore alone mars the lovely and tranquil prospect: the Club House. The late Victorians had a knack of doing the wrong thing… [constructing] a tall, narrow, lop-sided, defiantly hideous object." However, once safely inside, he succumbed to the "pleasant luncheons" and "coffee on the wide balcony overlooking the first tee and the last green" to the point where he found himself recalling with nothing but affection "a building that would have disgraced even Surrey."

On this particular day in the Smoke Room, a coal fire burns in the grate, casting a warm glow over the old lockers that line one wall. An almost palpable feeling of golfing fellowship and family friendliness greets the visitor. Wives and children, which in most clubs would be beyond the pale, are a fixture here. An octogenarian lady with a child in a stroller comes in; Nigel Carrington-Smith and Tom Harvey are sipping pink gins (the favourite Club drink) at the bar; John Coleridge, the Club historian and a poet, is explaining to a newcomer that betting has never been part of the Brancaster tradition ("Good Heavens," he exclaims, "you'd be drummed out if you did!"); pipe, cigar and cigarette smoke mingle, floating up to the Captains' boards at either end of the room.

Formal lunches and dinners are rare at Brancaster, card games non-existent, and evening events only on special occasions. People come to play golf and be with friends and indeed, treat the Club as an extension of their own homes. Nowhere is this informality more vividly reflected than in the lack of a dress-code. Nigel Carrington-Smith remembers being struck by it on his first visit to the Club.

"There was every kind of dress imaginable in the Smoke Room: gumboots, hats, coats, jackets, shorts. I asked the outgoing Secretary if he had to impose dress regulations. He snorted and almost fell out of his chair. 'Good God, no — but draw the line at bare feet.'"

An integral part of life at Royal West Norfolk is the canine community. At the entrance of the clubhouse are two large water bowls for dogs and it is unusual to see players on the course without dogs. One Captain used to take his five whippets out regularly and, until recently, dogs were allowed into the Smoke Room. But then a new carpet was installed, at some cost, and the dogs had to beat a retreat.

Pat Ward-Thomas, a loyal Brancastrian, deserves the final word: "The Club owns the freehold of the course itself, and so Brancaster can remain a place of peace for evermore. It has no call for progressives and eager beavers; the golfer is left alone." With, one should add, his family and his dogs.

A Hidden Gem

Royal Porthcawl Golf Club

From outside it looks like an army cantonment, of First World War vintage, which the government forgot to pull down, so you could be forgiven for thinking that an old comrades' reunion is taking place in the bar. There is a great clatter of glasses, shouts of laughter, and some energetic flexing of Welsh biceps. Roughly half the men drinking in the wood-panelled room with its golfing trophies and honour boards and ancient teak floor pitted by generations of golf spikes, are wearing ties with yellow, black and blue stripes. These are the Sparrows, Royal Porthcawl's special flock of golfers, birds of a feather known for their capacity for collective enjoyment, drinking prowess, and general derring-do.

The other half, who happen to be members of a visiting golfing society, are less flamboyantly attired and not as boisterous. But they're all having a good time after an enjoyable game of golf whose result, for the Sparrows if not for their opponents, was of considerably less importance than its speed of execution. This is a regular Wednesday event at Porthcawl: the Sparrows gather and either play a visiting society or amongst themselves on the Club's blustery but subtle seaside golf course. A convivial dinner helps to anchor the performance at the bar, then kummel and more liquid refreshment, followed by a late night session of liar dice for the hardcore in the card room. The scene in the Club car park the next morning — where cars have been abandoned, after several false starts, in all directions — records the intensity of the evening's entertainment more eloquently than words.

Porthcawl is off the beaten golf track. It lies twenty-five miles west of Cardiff and eighteen miles east of Swansea along the Bristol Channel, and is one of Wales's oldest and most famous golf clubs. With the modern bridge over the River Severn and the building of the M-4 motorway, which runs within three miles of the small seaside town of Porthcawl, the Club is no longer hard to reach. But it is not part of a cluster of fine links courses as say Hoylake or Prestwick and therefore does not attract the packaged golf tours. Nevertheless, as the Michelin Guide says of a notable but out-of-the-way restaurant, it is worth a detour.

It was founded in 1891 by Cardiff golfers who wanted a seaside course and settled in Porthcawl. The original 9 holes were laid out on Lock's Common by Charles Gibson, the professional at Westward Ho! in Devon. In 1895 the founders leased some shore-side land from nearby Morgan Abbey, and Ramsey Hunter laid out a proper 18-hole course. In 1909, the Club received its royal title from King Edward VII and later his grandson, the Prince of Wales (the future Edward VIII), became the Club's patron. The Prince's portrait, painted appropriately by Hal Ludlow, an outstanding Welsh amateur golfer, hangs in the Common Room at the clubhouse. (The only other royal golf club in Wales is Royal St. David's at Harlech in the north.)

The clubhouse, which began life as workmens' quarters in Queen Victoria's Diamond Jubilee Exhibition in Crystal Palace, London, was dismantled and reassembled at Porthcawl. Externally it has never lost its temporary barrack-room appearance, but it has withstood decades of constant use and the fierce winds and storms that roll up the Bristol Channel from the Atlantic Ocean. Lovingly re-clad and strengthened many times, this odd structure continues to preserve its quaint and friendly atmosphere within and forms a perfect foil for the beauty of the course it serves.

Strictly speaking Porthcawl is not a links course in that it was not built on land reclaimed from the sea and there is no line of protective sand dunes. But it has the appearance and feel of links land. The Atlantic Ocean barrels up the Bristol Channel producing immense tides of up to forty feet; the winds, south-westerly prevailing, are proportionately powerful; the sea threatens several holes; the underlying sand provides excellent drainage; and there are no trees. There is also a marvellous bonus that comes with the lack of dunes: you can see the sea from every hole.

If you want to get a good sense of what is in store, suck in a lungful of salty air, brace yourself against the wind, and take a brisk walk to the 6th tee which is directly across the course near the northern boundary. To the north-west lies the Gower peninsula and Swansea; westwards, across the Bristol Channel, are the hills of Exmoor in north Devon; and to the north-east Margam Mountain. Closer in is the stark and semi-ruined Sker House, originally a medieval grange built by Cistercian monks (and reputedly haunted by the ghost of a young woman who died of a broken heart in the last century); the Rest, a mid-nineteenth century convalescent home for coal-miners suffering from black lung disease; the Port Talbot steel refinery (not a pretty sight); and looking more military, more transient than ever, Porthcawl's endearing clubhouse.

It is wise not to be lulled into a false sense of security about the velocity of the wind just because the course is next to a "channel" which conjures up an image of sheltering banks. On the contrary, the coastline is fully exposed to the brunt of the Atlantic gales. The wind can be devastating: balls fly off the greens, flags blow out of their holes and, on one famous night in the winter of 1990, the professional's shop took off and its splintered remains were found the next morning all over the car park. Porthcawl's centenary history (1891–1991), compiled and edited by Leo McMahon, must be the only book of its kind which, among its wide-ranging and fascinating appendices, includes a list of shipwrecks in the area.

Previous pages:
A stiff breeze off the Bristol Channel.
Opposite:
Silver championship trophy.

Following pages:
Driving off the 16th hole with the haunting landmark of the Sker House beyond. Clubhouse gallery past and present. The Sparrows Golfing Society.

The first three holes that run close to the shore provide a special challenge not to put your ball over the out-of-bounds fence onto the beach and are under constant threat from a voracious sea. In compensation, Porthcawl enjoys a quirk in the weather system whereby storms and rain coming in from the Devon coast often divide, one section heading for Cardiff and the other going to Swansea, leaving the Porthcawl area relatively unscathed and in perfect fettle for golfers.

The course itself has been modified and improved over the years first by Harry Colt in 1913, then by Tom Simpson in 1933 and with some small changes in 1950 by C. K. Potter and finally in 1986 by Donald Steel. The latest course modification was forced by the sea attacking the green of the 2nd hole. An alternative green has been built further inland for normal use, although the original green will be used for competitions as long as it survives.

The Club, like many of its peers, has had very few professionals, only three in the first hundred years of its existence, the first sixty of which were accounted for by James Hutchinson ("Hutch"), who came down from Scotland at the Club's inception and died in harness in 1951. The present incumbent, Peter Evans, took over in tragic circumstances when his predecessor, Graham Poor, was killed in an air crash. Now 32, Peter Evans had worked at the Club earlier as an assistant and is an enthusiastic and eloquent guide to the multi-faceted qualities of this Welsh jewel of a golf course.

"It has many different moods, depending on the wind and the weather," he says. "The course doesn't run straight out and straight back as many championship links courses do. The first three holes go parallel to the shore then the course cuts back in on itself, looping and winding through the back nine, playing all sorts of directions with different winds. This is the greatest test of the course. You have to play all winds, cross-winds, down wind and into the wind."

"When you look at the yardage of a lot of the holes, they don't look that fierce. But they are very subtle. Length isn't always at a premium at Porthcawl, position of play is the great tactical aim. I think this is one of the great defences that this course has against modern golf technology where balls are being driven enormous distances. If I were to choose a signature hole it is the 2nd, a par 4. The shore is very close and even with the new alternative green, it takes the greatest nerve and skill to take the shot on. The golf broadcaster Bruce Critchley chose it as the best 2nd hole in golf, and I agree with him."

"Porthcawl changes in character as you go round," says John Downing, a former Captain. "When you get to the 5th or 6th hole you are no longer on a links course, the feel is different. And then later on, certainly by the 13th, you know jolly well that you are back on a links course. On the whole the professionals don't like it. But I think it is a marvellous foursomes course."

The Amateur Championship has been held at Royal Porthcawl on five occasions and the inaugural Welsh Amateur Championship took place on the links in 1900 and

Opposite: *Portrait of the Prince of Wales, royal patron of Porthcawl, in golfing attire, by Hal Ludlow. On seeing the painting for the first time, the future King Edward VIII supposedly commented: "It's a fine picture of a pair of shoes."*

Following pages:
The Sparrows choosing partners at their weekly get-together.

J. C. R. (John) Downing, former Club captain and Chief Sparrow.

many times since. The Club has also hosted the Dunlop Masters (Peter Thomson won it), three Coral Welsh Classics, several European team matches, the Walker Cup (in 1995), and in 1998 the home internationals (England, Scotland, Wales and Ireland) for the eighth time. An Open is not an option because of the difficulty in handling the crowds and equipment although the course itself could probably meet the challenge.

The bulk of Porthcawl's membership was traditionally from Cardiff and composed largely of men who tended to be involved with the great coal industry of South Wales when Cardiff was the leading exporter of coal in Europe. Cardiff still dominates the membership but there is now a far greater mix from other parts of South Wales and beyond. It currently numbers around 800, of whom 320 are full male members but only eighty or so are really active. There has always been a ladies' section and their presence in the spacious Common Room (known by the old guard as the "Snake Pit") and their own sitting-room, which has the best view of the course, is an integral part of the Club's history. There is a small junior section but, like many traditional

W. E. (Bill) Rhys, Club president, and Dr. L. (Leo) McMahon, former captain and Club historian.

golf clubs, the age profile at Porthcawl is already advanced and getting older.

The Club's policy is not to have people kicking their spikes for years in a golfing purgatory, so there is no waiting list, but membership is strictly by invitation only. The Club admits new members at a steady, if modest rate, but only after they have passed through a careful vetting process that involves meeting members of the committee and playing the course. There is no handicap qualification but with a potential new member, who is proving to be acceptable in all respects except his game, a few lessons with the Pro are tactfully suggested — and invariably taken.

The style of the Club is laid-back, warm and uncompetitive. "We're similar to Brancaster," says Bill Rhys, Porthcawl's president, "a little hidden, very united, a simple dress code, and very friendly." "To call this a competitive club would be a massive over-statement," says Peter Evans. "The average entry in our monthly medals is about eight to ten people." The game is foursomes with singles for medal and Stableford competitions. The good doctor, who joined Harry Vardon (the "Vardon Grip") by leaving his name on an aspect of the game, was a Porthcawl member.

Following pages: *On the green at the 2nd hole at high tide in the Bristol Channel.*

The Club does not have a particularly Welsh ethnic flavour but there is, as Leo McMahon suggests, something there. "Our reputation of being a friendly club is partly because it is a Welsh attribute." Porthcawl is proud of its role in the development of Welsh golf and it appeals to Welsh (and Wales-domiciled) sportsmen and sports writers, such as the rugby international Gareth Edwards and golf writers Tony Lewis (*The Daily Telegraph*), Peter Corrigan (*The Observer*) and John Hopkins (*The Times*).

The balance between members' play and visitors' rounds is firmly in the favour of the former. "About 20,000 rounds of golf are played here every year and of that roughly seventy-five percent is accounted for by the membership," says Tony Woolcott, the recently retired Club Secretary and now a member in his own right.

The Club's finances are healthy after considerable capital expenditure on a new shop for the professional (to replace the one that finished up in the car park), the Secretary's office, and a Dormy House which contains six single and three double bedrooms, a great boon given Porthcawl's location. (Of the twelve clubs covered in this book, only Porthcawl and St. George's have Dormy Houses).

Porthcawl is a club with sections but not divisions. The chirpy Sparrows, although perhaps giving the impression of being separate with their special ties, are in fact a good illustration of the homogeneity and harmony of Porthcawl. Anyone can be a Sparrow, you come and go as you please. The motto is "If You Win, You Lose" (win at golf or dice and you pay for the drinks, a Pyrrhic victory indeed in such company).

The Sparrows actually originated outside Porthcawl, as John Downing, a founding member, explains: "It was in the early 1960s when I was living and working in Cardiff. My golfing friends and I would get together on Wednesday afternoons, then the early closing day of the week, our minds turning away from girls towards golf. We tended to play at clubs around the Cardiff area and a tradition built up. We'd have bacon and eggs or whatever the Club offered after the game and would play liar dice late into the night. There were other forms of amusement too such as the game my brother, a schoolmaster, invented. You had to go round the bar in the clubhouse, clinging to the walls and without touching the floor. If you fell down you'd be instantly disqualified. One night someone fell off and an ambulance was called while he was laid out on the putting green. He was off work for a couple of weeks."

John Downing, who has a Churchillian delivery and a Shakespearean actor's sense of timing, pauses to sip his coffee. "We didn't play at Porthcawl then, too expensive, but came to settle there later in the decade," he continues. "It remained a Wednesday afternoon and evening affair and we started having matches with visiting societies. You'd always have a dozen or so people who'd stay behind, have dinner and play liar dice — and that's continued. The Sparrows have swept up most of the Club members in the middle age range during their time, and there is an affection for them here. But if the Sparrows disappeared, it wouldn't be serious, whereas if Porthcawl disappeared it would be a disaster."

Once a year, the Sparrows migrate for a weekend. The destination now varies but traditionally it used to be to Llandrindod, Radnorshire, in mid-Wales.

"Llandrindod Wells, the great spa town," says John Downing. "Dodge City."

Another pause prompting a question: "Was it a very jolly event?"

"Piss up."

"Any golf played?"

"With difficulty."

Porthcawl is closely associated with another, more decorous golfing society, the Erratics, which after an itinerant early life also settled at the Club. Bill Rhys, the president of Porthcawl, and Leo McMahon, the Club historian, are both former Captains of the Club and recorders of the Erratics. The society, they say, was founded in South Wales by members of the Glamorganshire Golf Club, the Cardiff-based club whose members were largely responsible for founding Porthcawl itself at the end of the last century.

"Fifty percent of the Erratics' members used to be from there but now ninety percent are from Porthcawl," says Bill Rhys. "What often happens is that people join the Club here after they have become members of the Erratics from elsewhere. We are different in style from the Sparrows. We have a dinner on Friday night, have a draw and sell the partner or players, rather like the Match Club. There are several similar golfing societies around Britain: the Hittites at Royal Liverpool, the Leatherjackets in Somerset, the Wigorns in the Midlands, the Moles and the Match Club in the London area. We play all these except the Match Club. There's another mob called the Pirates, coming down from East Lothian soon. And there's the Windcheaters from Northern Ireland, a ferocious lot."

Another regular group, who meet on Wednesday lunch-time, consists of older members who are out on the first tee by 12.30 pm, and back three hours later for tea and toast in the clubhouse. Tom King Davies and Ralph Evans, both spry, charming men in their early eighties, are regular members of this group. They stress the importance of being able to come down to the Club and to go directly out onto the course with a minimum of fuss and no start times or hanging about. "That was the original idea here," says Tom King Davies, "and that's the way we want to keep it."

Porthcawl is similar to other traditional golf clubs in Britain in that it firmly believes foursomes is the best way to play golf (sociable, a way of mixing up players, and speedy), with allowance made for singles in medal and tournament play; that something is radically wrong if members have to be given starting times on the tee; and that while the course should — indeed must — be shared with the wider word of golf as much as possible, certain days must remain sacrosanct for the membership. Members, young and old, feel it is an inseparable part of their birthright to be able to turn up at the Club, when they feel in the mood for a game of golf with their friends, and drive off without further ado, just as their fathers, grandfathers and great-grandfathers did before them. That is what the word "traditional" means to them.

"I spend six days of the week here and I still pinch myself when I come to work, when I look out over the course," says Peter Evans. "Today it is a little bit overcast and drizzly but it still has great beauty, it has beauty in every mood for me. I always feel I'm fortunate to be the Pro here. Porthcawl is a hidden gem."

Are You in the Hat Today?

The Royal County Down Golf Club

Let us step back to the year of grace, 1909, and onto a crowded platform in Queen's Quay Station, Belfast. It is a Saturday, a little before midday, and a large group of gentlemen is assembling. They are dressed in country clothes, tweeds and plus-fours, cloth caps and stout walking shoes; most of them are be-whiskered in the fashion of the day and each man has a set of golf clubs. The golfers surge towards the forward coach, a particularly elegant conveyance that still bears the royal coat of arms from the time when it was used by King Edward VII and his queen. The station clock strikes twelve and the guard blows his whistle. The train pulls away and is soon chugging along through the green Ulster countryside.

Inside the well-furbished coach, the golfers are settling down to games of bridge or poker; and pipes, cigars and cigarettes are alight. One member of the group is sitting apart, taking names out of an old red top hat and, with commendable concentration, crafting foursome matches out of the assembled company.

"Well, Mister Hat Man, what have you in store for us today, sir?"

"You bide your time, Billy. All will be revealed in the bar, at the appointed hour. And for your temerity in interrupting the Hat Man's most onerous deliberations, you may buy me a drink, sir!"

An hour after leaving Belfast, the train draws into the small country station of Newcastle, County Down. The golfers step down, sniff the sea air appreciatively, glance up at the looming Mountains of Mourne, a shimmering blue haze shrouding the regal Slieve Donard peak, and set off on foot for the nearby clubhouse. The caddiemaster and his caddies, who have met the train, bustle around loading up the golf bags onto handcarts and follow the golfers at a respectful distance. The country is at peace, the empire is intact, industry and business are thriving, and the Hat is about to begin.

The Golfers' Express and the railway tracks that carried it for many decades are long gone. But the tradition of the weekly "Hat" endures, not only as the central golfing and social event of the Royal County Down Golf Club, but also as its spiritual backbone. For if ever a golf club were tied to a single tradition, it is this one. Indeed, without the Hat, County Down, for much of its membership, would not be County Down.

So here we are on another Saturday, almost a century after the passing of that gracious Edwardian era, in the Members Bar, waiting for the ritual of the Hat to commence. Behind the bar is a phalanx of glasses, already primed with gin; Angostura Bitters, bottles of tonic water and slices of lemon line up in support. In the far corner sits Alan Cooley, the Hat Man, his head down, working on his matches. Like a medieval alchemist blending herbs and potions, the Hat Man mixes such important matters as handicaps, form, personality, and frequency of play.

Meanwhile, the large room fills up with members — industrialists, businessmen, judges, lawyers, doctors and professional men, mainly from Belfast, and displaying the same confidence, *joie de vivre*, and good humour as their golfing forebears on the train. The gins, interspersed with pints of Guinness and draught beer, disappear at an alarming rate. The lilting accents of Ulster and further south mingle; laughter gusts like an autumn gale; and happy faces say more than words. Here beats the heart of a true golf club in the collective body of a group of men for whom this weekly gathering is a time-honoured and well-loved ritual.

"I've been a member of over a dozen golf clubs in my time," says Alan Cooley, a scratch player for many years, "but here you have the opportunity of playing different people every week. You can go away for a couple of months and then phone in on a Saturday morning and put your name in the Hat. You don't have to worry about letting your regular partners down. You can just pop in and out whenever you wish. It's a great institution but it can only work when you have a core group of about forty players. A lot more, or a lot fewer, and it wouldn't be on."

The rules are simple. You telephone the Club by 11.30 am in the winter, noon in the summer, and put your name down. (There is no longer an actual Hat; the old red topper disappeared with the Golfers' Coach and the railway.) The Hat Man then gets to work — he has a couple of assistants to step in if he is absent — and posts the matches on the notice-board in the Club Room. Games are foursomes in winter and four-ball in summer with low and high handicappers being deliberately mixed up. If the numbers are not quite right, the Hat Man will ask the Club professional to provide an assistant to even it up. Players bet, but only a pound a game, never more, never less.

Does anyone ever challenge the Hat Man's selections? "Clearly there are people, as in any club, who are less happy with someone or other," says Alan Cooley. "But there is an unwritten rule here that the Hat Man is all-powerful and if he decides that Joe Bloggs and Fred Smith, who may not always regard one another with equanimity, are picked together, they accept and go out and play."

"We come from a fairly wide background," says David Nicholson, the Captain. "But we get to know each other playing golf in the Hat. I think it was P. G. Wodehouse who said golf was the best way to find out people's character because no other sport so quickly exposes the cloven hoof."

A new Hat Man is chosen on the advice of the out-going man and a general sounding out of members. There is no formal process but whoever is chosen is unquestioningly accepted by the membership.

The Hat attracts about fifty players during the summer and between twenty and thir-

Previous pages:
The spectacular Royal County Down links framed by the waters of Dundrum Bay, the Mountains of Mourne, and the resort town of Newcastle with the Slieve Donard Hotel's landmark tower.
Opposite:
Royal County Down's crested blazer patch (detail).

Following pages:
Looking northward to a member driving off the 9th tee.

Above: I. H. (Harry) McCaw, twice Club captain and a former captain of the R&A.
Opposite: S. A. G. (Alan) Cooley, Hat Man, preparing Saturday matches with relish.

ty in the winter. "There is a hard crust of people who come down, rain, hail or snow," says Henry Mercer, the Club's Honorary Secretary. "The numbers seem to vary for no reason at all. On the wettest day, you may well find the largest group. There's a mix of ages, as well as handicaps, some fellows in their twenties and thirties while our eldest regular is eighty-three."

It is now 12.45 pm. The Hat Man's selections, neatly written out, are on the noticeboard; the bar is a graveyard of empty gin glasses and pint tankards. The members are having lunch and soon will be heading out to the 1st and 10th tees. There are no official start times, yet everything seems to sort itself out without undue congestion. The Club runs three Hat-style events — two on Saturday, morning and afternoon, and one on Wednesday afternoon. The most popular (and the most liquid-inspired), is Saturday afternoon.

All the golf courses in this book have their own natural beauty; comparisons are difficult as well as perhaps invidious. But Royal County Down, it has to be said, is in a class of its own. The setting is a classic blend of upland, lowland, water, and modest human habitation. Presiding over it all are the majestic Mountains of Mourne which, in the words of Percy French's famous song, do indeed "sweep down to the sea". Then comes the water itself in the shape of the great blue arc described by the Bay of Dundrum, opening out to the Irish Sea. Next, the rolling links, the whins a blazing yellow in spring and the heather a mellow purple in autumn. And between the course and the mountains lies the small town of Newcastle, with its whitewashed walls, red roofs and grey church spires, and its landmark Slieve Donard Hotel, built in 1897, and surmounted by a square, red-bricked Victorian Gothic tower.

The component parts are lovely enough in themselves but stand back and view the canvas as a whole from, say, the elevated 4th tee on the Championship Course. What you see is the work of a master painter, a landscape that satisfies the rational senses with its proportions, colour and balance, yet, with its bold brushwork depicting ever-changing light and shade, rain and wind, never fails to tug at the emotions. There is nothing quite like watching the sun burst through a pewter sky, chase the shadows over the tawny flanks of Slieve Donard, and send a shaft of molten silver light down over the golf course. You are gazing at what must be the most beautiful golf course in the world.

Beneath the beauty lies the reality of a great golf course. The Championship Course has evolved as the Club grew and prospered. The most recent improvements, involving the 17th and 18th holes, made them both more difficult and more aesthetically pleasing. But from the very beginning, the course demonstrated its pure links pedigree — undulating, narrow fairways, small greens, winds variable in direction and force, abundant dunes covered in gorse and heather, and enviable drainage that permits play throughout the year, barring snow and ice. County Down also has a signature all its own, its distinctive, whiskery marram-fringed bunkers. In addition to these charms, there are the controversial blind shots. The Club brochure describes these as charming and eccentric. "Much is made of them," it says, "and the comments are usually negative. But as they are all tee shots, and none is at a par 3, their actual effect is limited."

Natural beauty and natural links do not mean an easy ride. County Down is one of the toughest golf courses in the world. Herbert Warren Wind, after playing here, said he

Opposite: *A winter golfer appraising his approach to the 4th green.*

Opposite: *J. G. (John) Edwards, former captain and Hat Man, addressing a Guinness before lunch.*
Above: *D. (David) Nicholson, captain, and H. B. (Henry) Mercer, Honorary Secretary of Royal County Down, with caddies at the 1st tee.*

regarded it as "the sternest examination in golf" that he had ever taken. Peter Dobereiner, the British golf writer, consistently placed Royal County Down at the top of his list of golf courses in Britain and Ireland.

The Championship Links, at a shade over 7,000 yards (par 71), provides the challenge while the Annesley Links, formerly the Second Course, at a little over 4,300 yards (par 67), presents a smoother but still testing run. Donald Steel, the golf course architect, was brought in recently to renovate and improve this course and the Club spent £400,000 on the work.

The foundation of County Down in 1889 owes its formal origins to the work of a group of golf enthusiasts in Belfast in the 1880s. During that decade, a number of clubs were founded in Ireland, including County Down. The land for the links belonged to the local nobility, Hugh, the fifth Earl of Annesley, who happily agreed to lease it and became the Club's inaugural president. The course received its first distinguished visiting player, a few months after opening its doors, in the shape of the redoubtable Horace Hutchinson. The clubhouse was built in 1897, and royal patronage, from King Edward VII, was bestowed in 1908.

The First World War cut a swathe through the Club's membership and included the death of its second president, Francis, the sixth Earl Annesley, an excellent golfer who

Following pages: *Recovery from the rough, 9th hole.*

Walking from the 7th green to the 8th tee on the Annesley Links.

Bunker with distinctive marram grass fringe.

Above: *The Club seal in marble and granite.*
Opposite top left: *Verses by Willie Haughton, illustrated by Huw Wallace, in the Club's original Suggestions Book.*
Opposite top right: *Lacing up in the changing-room.*
Opposite bottom left: *A pint of the Irish elixir.*
Opposite bottom right: *Club silver.*

Following pages: *Ninth hole approach.*

had succeeded his father as president in 1909. But the Club recovered and flourished in the 1920s and 1930s, when many important competitions were played. Like other traditional golf clubs, it suffered similar cycles of prosperity and difficulty during and after the Second World War until the modern era, when new strategies were adopted to preserve and improve the two courses and the clubhouse.

After the death of Earl Annesley, the Club had no more presidents but the family connection remains to this day through the active membership of Richard Annesley, who inherited the estates but not the title, which is extinct. He recently donated the freehold of the links to the Club which reciprocated by re-naming the Second Course in the Annesley family's honour.

County Down, along with Portmarnock, shares the distinction of being the only Irish club to have had a Captain of the R&A selected from its ranks. Harry McCaw is County Down's flag-bearer (Joe Carr is Portmarnock's). He received his call in 1995. No one could have been better qualified, having done everything that could be done at his own Club and much for Irish golf in general. He was Captain of County Down twice, first in 1970, and then again in 1989, the Club's centenary year.

Royal County Down has a distinguished record of competitive events. But there was some early dissatisfaction, at least in the Belfast press, with golf's ruling body over the sea in Scotland. The Club's interesting and witty centenary history, *The First Century*, written by Harry McCaw and Brum Henderson, quotes a trenchant editorial in the *Northern Whig* in 1902, complaining of the R&A's lack of appreciation of the course's championship qualities. "The truth is that the present course at Newcastle," wrote the newspaper, "has a range, as fine greens, and as noble hazards as the keenest golfer could desire, and the splendid scenery of the Mourne range is more to be desired than the flatlands of St. Andrews or the morass of Muirfield."

Four years after its foundation, the Club staged its first major championship, the Irish Open Amateur, which was won by John Ball of Hoylake, the greatest amateur golfer of his day. Many Irish Open and Close Amateur championships were to follow as well as the Irish Open Championship, on three occasions, and the Irish Professional Championship (four times). County Down hosted the home internationals in 1933 and 1957, and Michael Bonallack, now the Secretary of the R&A, had the distinction of winning the only Amateur Championship, in 1970, to be held at the Club.

Although Royal County Down is a traditional men's club, it is proud of its role in ladies' golf. The Ladies Club, a separate institution but sharing the courses, was founded in 1894 with the Countess Annesley as its first president. Four years later the Club held its first mixed foursomes during which one bold lady, noting it was leap year, proposed to her partner on the back of the programme. She ended her carefully drafted letter thus: "If I am wrong, let the matter rest, you keep your council and I'll keep mine, and if no answer upon the subject, I suppose I shall be at liberty to 'Pop the question' elsewhere." The Club history does not record the result of this non-golfing challenge.

County Down went on to host ten Irish Ladies Close Championships and seven Ladies British Open Amateur Championships. In 1968, the Curtis Cup was played over the links, the American team winning.

Royal County Down is a medium-sized golf club with a total of 480 members, including a number of "outport" members who reside more than fifty miles from the Club, juniors (eighteen to twenty-five years old), and a section of juvenile associates (under eighteen) who are mainly sons of members. "Membership is by invitation," says Peter Rolph, the Club Secretary. "There is no waiting as such and the annual turnover is pretty low, less than ten a year. The whole thing is measured by how many people we can reasonably get onto the course on members' days on Saturday for the Hat." (The fundamental criterion for a candidate for membership is simple: is he "Hatable"?)

Given that the maximum number playing in the Hat is no more than sixty, the turnout is a small proportion of the total membership and even lower on Wednesday, the only other day set aside exclusively for members. Sunday is reserved for the Mourne Club, which started as an artisans' club in 1946, and is now a thriving local group of some 300 members. The rest of the week is packed with visitors in summer, or deserted in winter.

The commercial side has become large in recent years. During the summer season, buses full of golfers, usually Americans on a package tour of famous Irish golf clubs, roll up to the Club and disgorge their occupants. The income is considerable and the Club has come to rely on it. The money has gone on the Annesley Course, sea defences, and keeping members' subscriptions at reasonable levels. Like Prestwick, the course has two faces, depending on the day of the week and the time of the year. At times the dichotomy appears a little stark as when the members' dining-room is partitioned off with a simple screen during a busy lunch time with the visitors having the larger section overlooking the course.

In general, however, a *modus vivendi* between the friendly, familiar face of members' days and the alien face of commercial endeavour seems to have been achieved. The bottom line is simple: is the Saturday Hat allowed to function in its time-honoured, carefree way, or not? The most fleeting glance into the Members Bar at 12.30 pm on any Saturday of the year will provide an unequivocal answer in the affirmative.

Perhaps surprisingly, Northern Ireland's political troubles have not cast much of a shadow over the Club or, indeed, over Irish golf which, like rugby football, remains organised on an all-Ireland basis. Throughout the most recent decades of "troubles", the Club had one incident, an IRA car bomb that blew up in the car park and injured the caddiemaster who happened to be walking around the side of the clubhouse at the time. Some of the members, who are in government service, are accompanied to the Hat by their bodyguards but the Club has no sectarian prejudices. The membership includes half a dozen Roman Catholic priests, who are keen golfers and popular members, and several "outport" members from the Republic.

The essence of Royal County Down is tolerance, homeliness and openness. "We are the custodians of one of the great golf courses of the world," says Harry McCaw. "We have an obligation to share it."

Members regard their Club with deep affection, a home away from home, a blessed retreat enhanced by a superb golf course surrounded by marvellous scenery. Buster Holland, a recent Captain of the Club and a loyal supporter of the Hat, put it simply. "When I was in practice as a gynaecologist, I would be working my butt off all week, and then come down here on Saturday. You meet the troops in the bar, have a couple of scoops, a nice lunch, go out and play golf on a lovely track. By the time I got home at seven o'clock in the evening, I felt that I'd just had a week's holiday."

Sanctuary

Portmarnock Golf Club

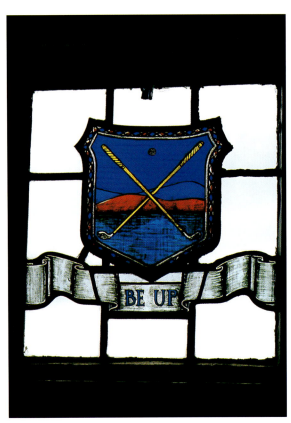

It is a Sunday morning in January and the reading on the wind recorder inside the Portmarnock Golf Club is "calm". But something is not quite right because outside members are bundled up like Alpine skiers; and on the links you can almost defy gravity by leaning into the north-westerly wind, which is gusting up to thirty miles per hour. The cold damp air seeps into your bone marrow. The rain has eased off but more is promised by billowing leaden clouds advancing over the sodden countryside. Perhaps it all has something to do with the old saying that in Ireland things are often critical but never serious. In any event, this famous golf course on the shores of the Irish Sea is bristling with golfers — cheerful, ruddy-faced Irishmen, humping their bags, their lilting voices and laughter carried on the wind.

"I've always felt that Portmarnock is the fairest test of the game of golf in the world," says Joe Carr, the leading amateur golfer in Ireland and Britain for many years and a veteran member of the Club. "You get exactly what you deserve and there are no bad breaks." He makes the point that Portmarnock, like all of the famous links courses, needs wind. Otherwise "they're murdered by the modern professional golfer. . . . The difference between wind and no wind here is probably six or seven shots."

The course has a natural symmetry and a serene beauty, despite the wind. It has water on three sides, great clumps of pine trees near the clubhouse — unusual on a links course — lovely views of Lambay and Ireland's Eye islands, the Hill of Howth to the south and, on a clear day, the Mountains of Mourne to the north-west, behind which nestles the Royal County Down Golf Club. The characteristics of the 7,321-yard (par 72) championship course are a configuration of two spiralling loops of 9 holes each; deep, tenacious rough that punishes over-ambition and indiscretion alike; some blind shots; and fine, impeccably honest greens.

"Portmarnock should be, as it always was, a natural test of golf, where you are competing against nature instead of man-made obstacles," says Jack Eustace, a former Captain and Honorary Secretary and, at a sprightly ninety, the Club's oldest member. "When our ancestors founded the course, they did not have the means to do any landscaping." Jack Eustace joined the Club seventy years ago when the only motive power was the horse. "It had to wear boots when cutting fairways to avoid damaging them. As this was our only method of grass-cutting or earth-moving, we did not much of either."

The creation of Portmarnock Golf Club follows a familiar pattern. As with St. George's, Brancaster, Hoylake and other traditional golf clubs in the Britain and Ireland, missionary Scots in pursuit of a small white ball were the responsible party. According to the Club history, it all started one day in 1894, when a twenty-six-year-old Scottish insurance broker in Dublin named William Chalmers Pickeman and his solicitor friend George Ross, rowed across the sea to the Portmarnock peninsula. They set foot on what they immediately recognised to be prime links land, a mere eight miles north of the centre of Dublin.

The property belonged to John Jameson and his family, also of Scottish origin, who had founded the famous whiskey distillery in Dublin in the eighteenth century and who had their own golf course nearby. In a twinkling of an eye, a deal was struck: a twenty-five-year lease, "on most moderate terms," was agreed and the Portmarnock Golf Club was officially established in October 1894 with John Jameson as its president, George Ross as Captain and William Pickeman Honorary Secretary and Treasurer.

Pickeman was the moving force behind the venture and he hired Mungo Park, from Scotland, to help him lay out the initial 9 holes (Park became the Club's first professional) and, later, George Coburn, another Scot, to craft the second 9. Much later, in 1971, a further 9 holes was added, designed by Fred Hawtree. The virtues of a 27-hole golf course are extolled by Maurice Buckley, Portmarnock's present Honorary Secretary. "It is, in my view, a great golf course because, no matter what is on, you can always get a game of golf. If, for example, there is a competition on the championship course, you can still play 18 holes through a combination of the third 9 and the old course."

Portmarnock was splendid in its isolation, a large and private peninsula with watery vistas in virtually every direction, yet it was not far from Dublin. Even at the turn of the century, the *Golfer's Magazine* noted that the journey, using "all the resources of civilisation — electric tram, train, outside car and boat," took less than an hour. When the tide was low, the golfers would finish their journey by riding across the muddy estuary, otherwise they had to take a boat from Baldoyle until a raised all-weather road was built.

The present clubhouse was built in 1906, a rather rambling Edwardian affair, which succeeded the original thatched cottage (a rented squatter's house) and a later custom-built edifice that burnt down. Its most interesting features are the club room, known in the Irish way as the Lounge, with an open fireplace, hanging lamps and deep leather armchairs, and one of the very few attractive locker-rooms in the pantheon of traditional golf clubs. Built in 1912, rows of navy blue lockers with brass door knobs are lit by natural light through skylights that run the length of the room; it is simple but, like the course, has a pure, natural feeling.

The Members Bar, again equipped with a cosy coal-burning fire, contains two curiosities. These are not the two gentlemen who, following their Sunday game, habitually drink and talk by the fireside until nightfall, but a pair of framed artefacts on the wall. One is a map of Howth and Conyborough [Portmarnock], dated 1800, drawn and

Previous pages:
Across the bay to the Hill of Howth.
Opposite:
Stained glass detail.

Following pages:
Early morning greenkeeping.

J. F. (Jack) Eustace, Portmarnock veteran. Opposite: View through caddiemaster's door.

signed by Captain William Bligh, RN, of HMS Bounty fame, and the other a letter from former US president George Bush, dated August 1991, on the eve of the Walker Cup at Portmarnock, a competition named after his maternal grandfather, George Herbert Walker.

Portmarnock, like Royal County Down, made an early and significant impact on Irish golf. Within a mere five years of its creation, the Club was hosting its first professional competition, which was won by Harry Vardon. Portmarnock was soon a regular venue for the Irish Professional Golf Association championships and, in 1927, the first Irish Open Championship was held there. This competition returned another five times, and Carroll's Irish Open was staged at Portmarnock no less than fourteen times between 1975 and 1990.

In 1995 a severe drought and the feet of the spectators following a succession of Irish Opens almost killed the course and it had to be closed. The Club turned down the tournament in 1996 but rest and irrigation have restored the links and they are now as good as they ever were.

Erosion by the sea, the bane of most links courses, has threatened the holes along the Velvet Strand on the upper part of the exposed eastern side of the peninsula. The 12th, 15th and 16th holes have been the most vulnerable, but the problem is under

Following pages: Chipping on to the 14th green.

Above: *J. B. (Joe) Carr, former captain of the Walker Cup team and of the R&A.*
Opposite top: *M. A. (Maurice) Buckley, Honorary Secretary.*
Opposite bottom: *The Portmarnock Lounge.*

Following pages: *A good out from the bunker on the 4th green.*

control and there is a compensatory land build-up at the lower end of the course. Flooding sometimes occurs on the links but, unlike Ireland's inland courses, the water drains away quickly and play goes on. Snow is rare and when it comes it soon melts.

The game at Portmarnock is four-ball and singles for competitions. As a member explained, "We have the sort of weather that allows us to play four-ball nearly all year." Foursomes, so popular in the Scottish clubs, the County Down "Hat" (at least in winter) and some of the smaller English clubs, are not often played. "The first rule when you play here is not to take any notice of the weather forecast. It may sound hopeless, but it's either wrong or the weather will change for the better before the day is out."

A strong competitive spirit manifests itself within the Club but not when it comes to playing other clubs and golfing societies. "Our custom in inter-club matches is to go out in the first round," said a member, "but club competitions are keenly contested, particularly around Christmas when we play for turkeys." Betting is modest or non-existent.

Club activities are centred on golf. The Captain's Dinner, the Christmas party and a small dinner after the Annual General Meeting are the only serious evening events. Formal lunches are not common either, most members preferring soup and sandwiches in the informality of the snack bar. Also, two institutions so much part of most traditional English golf clubs — the drinking of kummel and canine companions on the course — are absent. But, when it comes to liquid refreshment, the Irish are not short of a few ideas. In the bar all the Irish whiskeys are well-represented (Jameson, Powers, Paddy, Crested Ten, Black Bush and Bushmills Malt — Ireland's only single malt whiskey) and well used, not to mention Guinness and several fine draught beers, notably the divine Smithwick's. But surprisingly here too, the laws against drinking and driving have materially cut back on traditional merrymaking.

While Portmarnock has a generous share of emblematic figures and Club characters, the collective contributions of three members help to define the Club's historical trajectory, golfing pedigree and human flavour. These are Harry Bradshaw, Jack Eustace and Joe Carr.

Harry Bradshaw joined Portmarnock as its professional in 1950 and remained with the Club until his death in 1990. A Ryder Cup player who counted among his triumphs the Irish Professional Championship, the Irish Open and the Dunlop Masters, he also entered the "curious and sad events" annals of golfing legend at the British Open at Royal St. George's in 1949, when, at the 5th hole, his tee shot landed in a broken bottle. Rather than wait for a decision, he went on and played the shot, sending the ball only about twenty yards amid much flying glass and taking him another four shots to hole out. He eventually finished level with Bobby Locke, only to lose in the play-off. "The Brad", as he was fondly known, was a much-loved

Opposite top: *Joe Carr and friends.* Opposite bottom: *Members driving off the 1st tee.*

Following pages:
Rough around the 6th hole Yellow Nine.
At dawn near the clubhouse.

figure at Portmarnock as teacher, raconteur and role-model for the young.

Jack Eustace, who joined Portmarnock as a juvenile member in 1925 and has served as Captain, Honorary Secretary and president, provides an extraordinary human link to the foundation of the Club with his vivid memories of William Pickeman. "I remember him as a tall, heavy man, a bright red face adorned by glasses and a full moustache, drooping at the sides," he writes in an interesting personal account of the Club. "Pickeman was a very good scratch player," as well as a great coiner of golfing aphorisms, one of which is quoted in the Club history: "Don't forget at all times to talk as loudly as possible both on the links and in the clubhouse. It commands attention, and although many will consider you a cad, others will accept you at your own evaluation."

Two things are special about Portmarnock for Jack Eustace. "First is the isolation. You're working away in Dublin and then you come out here — I remember people crossing the estuary in horse and carts — and you're back to primitive nature. The second thing is the members. People are only elected to the membership if they are clubbable. Money or power doesn't count." The blue eyes glisten with delight. "We've turned down several ministers of state." It may also be noted that religion plays no part in determining suitability for membership.

Jack Eustace is a traditionalist who believes that any good private members' club should be run by an autocracy or, as he put it, "a cell." He also firmly believes that Portmarnock should retain its status as a men's club. Ladies can play the course as guests and the Club hosts ladies' competitions and matches but there is no ladies' section. Jack Eustace's imprint on the Club also has a physical dimension. An amateur cabinet-maker of some skill, he made some of the honour boards, a few tables and the Captain's chair — an impressive throne-like structure of carved oak. "Well, I must go," he says rising to his feet. "It's my son's twenty-fifth wedding anniversary and I'm cooking dinner tonight for twelve people."

Joe Carr, now seventy-six and still playing golf regularly, is equally lively and full of Club lore and golfing memories from his brilliant amateur career. His father and mother were Portmarnock's manager and manageress, who lived on the premises, and young Joe spent the first seventeen years of his life there, playing all his early golf on the course. "I used to play every day and sometimes miss school to do so," he says. In the 1950s and 1960s, Joe Carr became "Mr. Amateur Golf" in Ireland and Britain, winning virtually everything in sight and captaining the Walker Cup team.

Joe Carr's contribution to the game was recognised in 1992 when the R&A honoured him as the first Irishman to be chosen as Captain of that august institution. During his captaincy he was once asked to referee a match at Pebble Beach in the United States. The local official's somewhat tenuous grasp of geography led to Joe Carr's duties being announced like this: "The referee for this match will be Mr. J. B. Carr, Captain of the Royal and Ancient Golf Club of St. Andrews in Scotland from Dublin, England." A friend, who was standing at his side, turned to him and said: "Wars have been started for less than that."

Portmarnock has a total of 1,100 members, of whom about half are full playing members. There is a juvenile section (twelve to sixteen years old) and a junior one (aged sixteen to twenty), as well as country, five-day and overseas members. Dublin is the home of the active membership, the southern part of the city accounting for sixty percent and the northern portion taking care of the rest. The average age is in the mid-sixties ("Jack Eustace brings us up a bit," laughs Joe Carr, no spring chicken himself.) The Club does not believe in waiting lists. "We're not worried about the Club dying out," says Maurice Buckley, "but we could have a serious problem in a few years time." The system is to open the door every decade or so and bring in a batch of new members. "We haven't had an election since 1990, when we let twenty people in. We might have another one in the next two years and again we'd be looking at about twenty new members."

Portmarnock is something of a national institution. Its honorary members include the President of Ireland, the US Ambassador, and other distinguished political figures. Visitors may play the course on Mondays, Tuesdays, Thursdays and during specific hours on Fridays. Societies are also welcome and all visitors, properly attired (jackets and ties) may go into the Members Bar and have lunch in the dining-room. But at Portmarnock there is no mass invasion with buses and supporting infantry as there are at many other Irish clubs.

As befits a national icon, the Club has a large and powerful hierarchy run, in effect, by that peculiarly Irish institution, the Honorary Secretary. In addition there is a Captain, president, two vice-presidents, an honorary treasurer, two trustees and an eight-man committee — more, one is tempted to say, than the entire playing membership of Swinley Forest.

The Honorary Secretary is chosen by the members and these days serves for five years. "If he's a strong character — and we've had quite a few who were — his word is law," says Joe Carr.

"The Honorary Secretary is basically your Managing Director, and is, generally speaking, traditional and conservative by nature. His general brief is to oversee Club policy and maintain the status quo. Inevitably, he has to make decisions that are not always popular and has, therefore, to be a strong character. Portmarnock has been fortunate to have had a history of very strong Honorary Secretaries, each with his own style, who have given tremendous service to the Club."

What does Portmarnock mean to the Irish? In a booklet celebrating the Club's first fifty years, published in 1944, Seamus O'Connor provided a response which still rings true. "To a thoughtful Irishman, Portmarnock means more than a golf links with a national and international reputation. . . . There one sees a harmonious union of Irishmen, a fusion of different ideas and different antecedents . . . friendships which might seem incongruous but are sincere and lasting [and] have grown and grown naturally."

A member, nursing his drink in the Lounge on that cold, windy Sunday, put it this way: "I remember one day a young barman asked me what Portmarnock was like and I told him it was not the sort of place where you get a pint thrown over you. It's a place, as we say in Ireland, that would put manners on you. It has a quiet, calming influence. It's a refuge."

Capital Golfers
The Golf Match Club

St. James's Street, London. It is a Thursday in late January in the heart of London's club-land. Half a dozen men in dinner jackets emerge from White's, turn left and walk down the street. Their destination is another fine Georgian building on the same side of the street. They turn into Boodle's and go up the grand staircase to the upper bar where a large group of similarly attired men have congregated. They greet each with pleasure for they are part of a brotherhood that is at once universal and particular; they are drawn together by the ancient game of golf, by their affinity for each other; and by their physical proximity in the capital where most of them live. Their purpose is to dine, arrange golf matches, bet on them and, very soon, to play them out before they meet here again.

The Match Club has recently celebrated its centenary. It is the oldest golf dinner match club in existence. It has no golf course, no clubhouse, no staff. Boodle's, where members meet on the third Thursday of every month from October through April, is the nearest thing the group have to a headquarters. The key to making this unusual Club work is the Recorder, of whom there have only been nine in more than a century. Simon Radcliffe, the present incumbent, took over in 1989 to, as his predecessor put it, "expand the sheer fun of Match Club dinners and golf." All the evidence indicates he has been highly successful.

The Recorders over the years have kept meticulous records of every match made by members of the Club. Thus, should one wish to know, one can ascertain that on 9 December 1956, in a match at the Berkshire, "Sir James Waterlow and the Hon. P. Samuel beat H. Ingram and Lord Tennyson" by one hole.

In earlier years Woking was the course of choice for most matches, with an occasional contest at the Berkshire or Swinley or Royal St. George's. These last three are prominent venues today, along with Sunningdale and occasionally Royal Ashdown Forest — or New Zeland. Woking has virtually disappeared. The location of the matches tends to reflect where Match Club members typically belong but, in theory, a match could be anywhere. While the membership is mostly from the London area, probably every club in this book has had a member in the Match Club.

The game is normally foursomes, played on level terms, over 36 holes at a mutually agreed golf course. But there can be other forms of play. Winners of matches traditionally pay for the lunch and tea at the Club where the match takes place. Matches, for Club stakes of £25 (plus side bets), must be played not later than the Sunday preceding the next dinner, at which all stakes and bets not already paid have to be settled. "Since the winners pay for lunch, things pretty much even out in the end, which is how it should be," says Simon Radcliffe. In the 1997–98 season the Club had seven dinners, fifty-six matches and

£17,060 was wagered. The dinners are growing in popularity, especially among the younger members, with an average turn-out of thirty-five a dinner.

There are seventy members, a Captain elected annually, the Recorder who organises the dinners, makes the matches and records the bets placed on them, and a committee of five. The Club, like all good golf clubs, has its own silver, albeit in modest amounts: four ancient putters hung with silver balls, presented by each retiring Captain, a silver butter dish and a silver fruit bowl. When not in use, these artefacts are stowed away in Boodle's safe.

The whole thing began in 1896 when Ernest Lehmann, an enthusiastic golfer and gentleman of leisure, thought it would be a good idea to start a dinner match club in London after attending a dinner at Muirfield where matches were made and bet upon. The first Match Club dinner was held in January 1897 at the Bath Club in Dover Street, Piccadilly; nineteen members attended, a Recorder and a Captain were elected, nine matches were made and nineteen pounds and fifteen shillings wagered. The Club history, published in 1996, notes that the Recorder wrote about the occasion: "At a late hour the members separated, the general feeling being that the inaugural dinner of the Club gave excellent promise of a successful and useful career for the new venture." Adding a comment of its own, the Club history observed: "Six hundred and forty-five dinners and four thousand, five hundred and fifty-six matches later, we are confident that... our three Founders would have shared our delight that it has indeed had a successful and useful career. So far . . . ."

Although small and exclusive, Match Club membership has always reflected the wider world of British golf as well as the loftier peaks of the British establishment, including Amateur champions Horace Hutchinson, Freddie Tait, Cyril Tolley, Robert Harris and Roger Wethered; Bernard Darwin was Captain (1906–07); and later, Arthur Croome, who helped found both the Oxford and Cambridge Golfing Society and the Senior Golfers' Society, was first Recorder (1919–23) and later Captain (1925–26).

The Match Club counts more than forty internationals among its membership, of whom thirteen have played in the Walker Cup, with eight of those as Captain of the team. Twenty-two R&A Captains have been Match Club members.

The Club has met and dined in many places — White's, the Turf Club, the Bath Club, the Carlton Hotel, the Café Royal and Claridge's amongst others — until coming to rest in the spacious elegance of Boodle's Club about twenty years ago.

In addition to members' matches, the Club also plays occasional matches against other golf clubs around the country and overseas. One of the regular and most popular fixtures is with Muirfield, the original source of inspiration for the London club. The Club history records that in 1994 the Match Club presented the Honourable Company with a case of Bollinger champagne to celebrate its 250th anniversary. The Match Club lost that encounter on the links, but retrieved its honour by drinking more of its gift than its recipients, "particularly at breakfast the day after the match."

Who are today's members of this unusual Club? They mostly belong to the R&A and traditional golf clubs in south-eastern England, notably Sunningdale, Royal St. George's, Swinley Forest and Rye. Family connections are strong, and their background is public school, most prominently Eton and Charterhouse. In the past the military, peers of the realm and parliamentarians were common, but today the legal profession and activities associated with the City of London predominate although there are a few members who, taking their cue from the Match Club's founding father, are gentlemen of leisure.

"The Match Club is a place of great fellowship, great bonhomie," says a rare American member. "The quality of golf is less important than the quality of the individual. They are a very classy lot. Straight out of central casting."

"It is a quintessential English institution," says Bruce Critchley, the golf writer and commentator. Membership is by invitation and the decision on a person's candidacy has to have the unanimous approval of the Club's five-man committee. A member who fails to turn up to at least one dinner during the season automatically forfeits his membership. Members who leave Britain may go on a non-active list and are welcome to join the dinners when visiting London. Guests may be brought to the dinner and play in the matches.

A word on the Moles, another London-based, golf-dinner-match club that is often viewed as a rival of the Match Club. The Moles were actually founded by a member of the Match Club (Victor Longstaff) in 1911, and there is a cross-over membership between the two clubs, so how do you know one from the other? "The Moles select their members from good golfers who dine," says Simon Radcliffe, "and the Match Club selects its members from good diners who play golf." Another definition comes from a stalwart who is a member of both clubs. "Moles shout *before* they're drunk," he says.

Dinner is almost over for the thirty Match Club members and their guests seated around the polished mahogany table in Boodles' magnificent candle-lit dining room, known prosaically — and misleadingly — as the Saloon. The damask curtains are drawn over the great Venetian window that faces St. James's Street and there is no intimation of the bitter night outside or the denizens of the vast city around them. Andrew Milne, the Captain, gets to his feet, followed by the rest of the diners. "Gentlemen, the Queen," he says, raising his glass. "The Queen," rumbles around the table as glasses are raised and the loyal toast drunk.

There is a short pause in the proceedings as members make a pit-stop to accommodate refreshment taken and to allow for more to come. Reassembled, Havanas are lit. Soon the group is enveloped in the rich aroma of pure, hand-rolled tobacco. Port and brandy circulate as the Captain invites the Recorder to read out the results of the previous dinner match and to confirm that all debts have been settled. He then welcomes the guests and announces the six matches made for this occasion, which members have made over drinks before dinner between themselves or occasionally with a guest. These have been written down on bits of paper earlier and tossed into the Club's silver fruit bowl. The Recorder must find that the match presents a fair bet; otherwise he will not announce it. When the Recorder calls out the matches betting ensues at a furious pace. It is meticulously recorded, notwithstanding the rigors of the evening's entertainment. After dinner members divide, some going upstairs to play snooker, others descending for a rubber of bridge or crossing St. James's Street for a final glass of port at Pratts. A few will move on to sample the late night activities of London.

Over a hundred years have passed since the first meeting of the Match Club, when Queen Victoria was still on the throne. A new century beckons as the members, laughing and joking, looking forward to the golf ahead, spill out onto St. James's broad thoroughfare. The cigar smoke swirls upwards and dissipates in the dark, cold air. They say a last goodnight and go their separate ways.

Match Club members and their guests drinking, dining and making matches at Boodle's, London.

Club Addresses

Royal and Ancient
Golf Club of St. Andrews
St. Andrews, Fife KY16 9JD,
Scotland
Tel: 01334-472112
Fax: 01334-477580
International Calls: 44-1334-472112

Prestwick Golf Club
2 Links Road,
Prestwick, Ayrshire KA9 1QG,
Scotland
Tel: 01292-477404
Fax: 01292-477255
International Calls: 44-1292-477404

Royal Liverpool Golf Club
Meols Drive,
Hoylake,
Wirral, Merseyside L47 4AL,
England
Tel: 0151-632-3101
Fax: 0151-632-6737
International Calls: 44-151-632-3101
E-Mail: Sec@rlgc.u-net.com

The Royal St. George's Golf Club
Sandwich, Kent CT13 9PB,
England
Tel: 01304-613090
Fax: 01304-611245
International Calls: 44-1304-613090

Rye Golf Club
Camber,
Rye, East Sussex TN31 7QS,
England
Tel: 01797-225241
Fax: 01797-225460
International Calls: 44-1797-225241

Sunningdale Golf Club
Ridgemount Road,
Sunningdale, Berkshire SL5 9RW,
England
Tel: 01344-21681
Fax: 01344-24154
International Calls: 44-1344-21681

no tie

Swinley Forest Golf Club
Coronation Road,
South Ascot, Berkshire SL5 9LE,
England
Tel: 01344-874979
Fax: 01344-874733
International Calls: 44-1344-874979

*Royal Worlington and
Newmarket Golf Club*
Mildenhall,
Bury St. Edmunds, Suffolk IP28 8SD,
England
Tel & Fax: 01638-717787
International Calls: 44-1638-717787

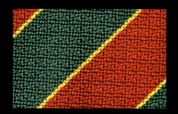

Royal West Norfolk Golf Club
Brancaster,
King's Lynn, Norfolk PE31 8AX,
England
Tel: 01485-210223
Fax: 01485-210087
International Calls: 44-1485-210223

Royal Porthcawl Golf Club
Porthcawl, Mid Glamorgan CF36 3UW,
Wales
Tel: 01656-782251
Fax: 01656-771687
International Calls: 44-1656-782251

The Royal County Down Golf Club
Newcastle, County Down BT33 0AN,
Northern Ireland,
UK
Tel: 013967-23314
Fax: 013967-26281
International Calls: 44-13967-23314

Portmarnock Golf Club
Portmarnock, County Dublin,
Ireland
Tel: 846-2968
Fax: 846-2601
International Calls: 353-1-846-2968

The Golf Match Club
No fixed address.
The monthly Match Club dinners are
held at Boodle's Club in London.

Acknowledgments

This book began with a question from my great friend, Richard Sutton: "Would you *ever* consider doing a book on golf?" Naming contributors, friends and associates who made this book possible is a distinct pleasure for me — though I began the project as a non-golfer, I have now "broken 100" a few times, and I am indebted to these people for giving me a new avocation . . . with minor injuries.

Richard Sutton and Brooks Carey, both keen golfers, have been my mentors throughout the preparation of this book. First traveling with me to Britain and Ireland to present the book concept to the Clubs, guarding against any errors in golf-talk, they later guided both author John de St. Jorre and me through the doors of the Clubs and out onto the golf courses to examine the ancient sport. Their reading of the text in progress was essential to the integrity of the project, and they were also very useful viewed through a long lens as very small people with clubs.

A large debt is owed to the Captains, Honorary Secretaries, past Captains and illustrious members who welcomed us into their Clubs with grace and good humor: Michael Attenborough, John and Shirley Batt, David Beazley, John Behrend, A.D.H. (Tony) Biggins, John Boardman, Tim, Liz and Alex Boatman, Michael J.E.G. Bower, Maurice Buckley, Nicholas Burn, J.B. (Joe) Carr, Bruce Chritchley, Richard Cole-Hamilton, S.A.G. Cooley, F.J. (Frank) Davis, J.C.R. (John) Downing, The 19th Earl of Derby, J.G. Edwards, J.E. (Jack) Eustace, Brian Fitzgerald, the late J.A. (Jo) Floyd, Margaret Freethy, F.R. ("Bobby") Furber, Peter Gardiner-Hill, Douglas Gardner, John R. Gillum, Gareth Griffiths, Daniel Griggs, Paul Guest, Neil Harman, David and Kathleen Harvey, Tom Harvey, Buster Holland, Dr. D.W. (David) James, John R. James, Jonathan and Sarah Jempson, Murray Lawrence, Peter Lewis, Ian Lochhead, Dr. Omar Malik, J.M. (Michael) Marshall, Sandy Mathewson, Harry McCaw, Dr. L. (Leo) McMahon, H.B. (Henry) Mercer, Sir John Milne, R.J. Morgan, Brian Morrison, D. (David) Nicholson, Ian Pattinson, Simon Radcliffe, W.E. (Bill) Rhys, R.C. (Rupert) Ross, Nicholas Royds, Michael Scott, Sir Patrick Sheehy, Tim Smartt, E.W. ("Jim") Swanton, Dr. A.D. (Percy) Walker, Stephen Walton and family and John Whitfield.

Special thanks are due to the Secretaries of the Clubs for their splendid effort: Sir Michael Bonallack, Ian Bunch, Major Nigel A. Carrington-Smith, Lt. Col. C.J. Gilbert, Major Guy Hipkin, Group Captain C.T. Moore, Colonel Ian T. Pearce, Frank Prescott, John Quigley, Peter Rolph, Gerald E. Watts, A.W. (Tony) Woolcott and Stewart Zuill.

It has been a pleasure to work with writer John de St. Jorre and designer Sam Antupit again; this is our third collaboration.

Ektachrome and Kodachrome film was generously provided by the Eastman Kodak Company; film processing by BWC Labs. Cameras and lenses were provided by Canon U.S.A. I also would like to acknowledge the following people for their time, generosity and friendship: Bill Acquavella, Anthony Adams, The Brook Club, Bill Caler, Nicholas Calloway, James Cowperthwait, Parker Gilbert, Cathy Harrison, Clifford Jones, Vicki Lewis, Mike Newler, Geoffrey Norman, John Phelan, Tim Smith, Karen Teitlebaum and Dick Wilson.

Lastly, no book of this size and scope could have been done without our generous sponsors: B.T. Alex Brown, Business Week Magazine, Canon U.S.A., Omni Hotels, Rolex Watch U.S.A. and U.S. Trust.

Anthony Edgeworth
Wellington, Florida
August 31, 1998

Edgeworth Editions
www.greatgolfcourses.com
1-877-360-golf